LIVES

OF THE

TWELVE APOSTLES:

WITH

EXPLANATORY NOTES.

BY F. W. P. GREENWOOD,
JUNIOR MINISTER OF KING'S CHAPEL, BOSTON.

'The glorious company of the Apostles praise Thee.'

BOSTON:
HILLIARD, GRAY, LITTLE, AND WILKINS.
MDCCCXXVIII.

Kessinger Publishing's Rare Mystical Reprints

THOUSANDS OF SCARCE BOOKS ON THESE AND OTHER SUBJECTS:

Freemasonry * Akashic * Alchemy * Alternative Health * Ancient Civilizations * Anthroposophy * Astrology * Astronomy * Aura * Bible Study * Cabalah * Cartomancy * Chakras * Clairvoyance * Comparative Religions * Divination * Druids * Eastern Thought * Egyptology * Esoterism * Essenes * Etheric * ESP * Gnosticism * Great White Brotherhood * Hermetics * Kabalah * Karma * Knights Templar * Kundalini * Magic * Meditation * Mediumship * Mesmerism * Metaphysics * Mithraism * Mystery Schools * Mysticism * Mythology * Numerology * Occultism * Palmistry * Pantheism * Parapsychology * Philosophy * Prosperity * Psychokinesis * Psychology * Pyramids * Qabalah * Reincarnation * Rosicrucian * Sacred Geometry * Secret Rituals * Secret Societies * Spiritism * Symbolism * Tarot * Telepathy * Theosophy * Transcendentalism * Upanishads * Vedanta * Wisdom * Yoga * *Plus Much More!*

DOWNLOAD A FREE CATALOG
AND
SEARCH OUR TITLES AT:

www.kessinger.net

DISTRICT OF MASSACHUSETTS, TO WIT:

District Clerk's Office.

BE it remembered, that on the twenty-second day of May, A. D. 1828, in the fifty-third year of the Independence of the United States of America, HILLIARD, GRAY, LITTLE, AND WILKINS, of the said district, have deposited in this office the title of a book, the right whereof they claim as proprietors, in the words following, to wit:

'Lives of the Twelve Apostles: with Explanatory Notes. By F. W. P. GREENWOOD, Junior Minister of King's Chapel, Boston. "The glorious company of the Apostles praise Thee."'

In conformity to the act of the Congress of the United States, entitled 'An act for the encouragement of learning, by securing the copies of maps, charts, and books, to the authors and proprietors of such copies, during the times therein mentioned;' and also to an act, entitled 'An act supplementary to an act, entitled, "An act for the encouragement of learning, by securing the copies of maps, charts, and books, to the authors and proprietors of such copies, during the times therein mentioned;" and extending the benefits thereof to the arts of designing, engraving, and etching historical and other prints.'

JNO. W. DAVIS,
Clerk of the District of Massachusetts.

EXAMINER PRESS.
Hiram Tupper, Printer—Bromfield Lane.

TO

THE MEMBERS

OF THE

SOCIETY WORSHIPPING AT KING'S CHAPEL,

THIS VOLUME,

WRITTEN FOR THEIR USE,

AND PUBLISHED AT THEIR REQUEST,

IS AFFECTIONATELY DEDICATED

BY THE AUTHOR.

LIVES OF THE APOSTLES.

INTRODUCTION.

Jesus Christ, the Saviour and Teacher sent from God, soon after he commenced his ministry, selected twelve men to be his immediate followers and confidential disciples. 'Now the names of the twelve apostles are these; the first, Simon who is called Peter, and Andrew his brother; James the son of Zebedee, and John his brother; Philip, and Bartholomew; Thomas, and Matthew the Publican; James the son of Alpheus, and Lebbeus, whose surname was Thaddeus; Simon the Canaanite, and Judas Iscariot, who also betrayed him.' This list of the apostles is taken from the Gospel of Matthew,* who was himself one of them. We are also presented with a similar catalogue in the Gospels of Mark and Luke, and in the book of Acts.

Why the exact number of twelve was appointed, it is more difficult than important to determine. Perhaps it was done in compliance with the attachment of

* Chap. x. 2, 3, 4.

the Jews to that number. Perhaps it was with a more particular reference to the number of the sons of Jacob, and the tribes of which they were the progenitors and founders; 'ye also,' says Jesus, 'shall sit upon twelve thrones, judging the twelve tribes of Israel.' This is a point, however, of little or no consequence; and therefore need not detain us in discussion.

The motives which induced the Master to call to himself a select company of disciples, seem to be much more obvious. It was proper and even necessary, that he should have some followers in whom he might particularly confide, and who should be always near him and about him.

It was needful, in the first place, that he should be thus attended, in order that the wonders, which he worked in confirmation of the divinity of his mission, should be nearly inspected and credibly attested. I deem it one of the strongest evidences of the truth of our Saviour's miracles, that they were performed, not only in sight of the multitude, but of a select company, who were too familiar with him to be deceived themselves, and too honest to join with him in deceiving others. Being brought into the midst of his operations, they were qualified to judge of their reality and integrity, and therefore qualified to report them to the world with all the warmth of conviction, and all the directness, particularity, and authority of constant experience and repeated vision. A changing crowd, never composed perhaps on any two occasions of the same materials, might have been mistaken; but a band of twelve companions could not have been. They were fitted, as in no other way they could have been so well, for the purpose of declaring to men the power from above with which their Master was invested; and that they might be thus prepared, was one of his designs in choosing them. 'Ye are *witnesses* of these things,' said he to the eleven, after his resurrection from the dead. He evinced a consciousness of innocence and sincerity, by admitting so many partakers of his secret counsels and his daily deeds; and he manifested his wisdom, by securing such an irrefragable testimony to the reality of those signs from Heaven, which pointed him out as truly the Son of God.

The apostles were selected, in the second place, in order that by reiterated instruction they might become well acquainted with the religion which their master was about to establish on the earth. 'It is given unto you to know the mysteries of the kingdom of heaven.' Jesus addressed himself to all who had ears to hear, but more particularly to those twelve, who were to preach in his name when he should be lifted up; because, through them, mankind were to receive the tidings of his salvation. He chose them, that he might teach them, so that they in turn might teach. His doctrine was so new, so different from what men had been used to dignify with the title of religion, that occasional lessons to the multitude, uttered in a confined sphere and by a single individual, would hardly have served the purpose of rendering it familiar and making it well understood. On this account it was more minutely, clearly, and repeatedly explained to a select class of pupils, who were thus prepared to become instructers themselves, and, by penetrating into different and distant countries, to disseminate among the nations of the earth a religious system, which was at first promulgated to the Jewish people, and limited to their small inheritance alone. They were called *apostles*, because they were *sent* out into the world. Before they were sent, they were instructed in the purposes and powers of their mission. And how slow they were to comprehend, after all the pains which had been bestowed on them, the true nature of the Messiah's kingdom and laws, may be read in their own confessions of ignorance. It was late, and not till after supernatural illumination, that they were thoroughly initiated in the true meaning of the religion, which they were committed to preach and to spread. This is a fact which forcibly attests, not the dullness of the disciples, for their natural perceptions were as quick as those of other men, but the need there was of their being well grounded in the doctrines of Christ, and the opposition which existed between the entire simplicity and spirituality of those doctrines, and the grossness of their own expectations and of the common opinions of the world.

It may be well to add to the above reasons for the separation of the twelve, that they were brought into a close personal intimacy with the Saviour, in order that they might study his example, borrow his spirit, and so receive the image of his life that they might reflect it in their own. They were both the witnesses and the objects and recipients of that divine gentleness, compassion, and benevolence, which from that fountain flowed out all abroad on every thing. They could not be so much in his society, without being affected by the bland influences of his manners and character. It was very probably intended that they should be thus affected; that they should behold the temper of Christianity in a living form; its doctrines set forth in conduct; its precepts illustrated by a perpetually corresponding practice; and that, beholding this, they should be touched by its beauty, and conformed in some measure to its likeness, and enabled to hold up, not only the description, but the copy of it, before the sight of men. It was almost an inevitable result of their situation, that they should imbibe a portion of the divine life of Christianity from their strict fellowship with its founder. Like those flowers, which are known to drink in the light of the sun while he remains above the horizon, and then to give it out in mild flashes when the evening shades come on, so the disciples, while their Master sojourned with them, while the sun of righteousness shone upon them, absorbed the beaming excellence of his character, and then, when he left the earth, emitted it partially again amidst the moral darkness which surrounded them.

One other purpose, which the connexion of the twelve disciples with our Saviour was fitted to answer, was, the qualification which it conferred on them for recording his deeds and words, and preserving to posterity the invaluable memorial. I know not how we, of this age, could have trusted implicitly to accounts of the origin and true principles of the christian religion, which tradition alone might have brought down to us; nor is it easily conceivable how any persons could have been better prepared to render an authentic, trustworthy, and interesting history of our faith, than were those who accompanied Jesus through the several scenes of his ministry, and immediately succeeded him in publishing the gospel. Accordingly, we find that two, out of the four, relations of our Saviour's life and death, were written by two of the twelve disciples; and that the greater part of the remaining books of the New Testament were likewise composed by the original apostles, and by that distinguished individual whose apostleship was bestowed on him directly and miraculously from Heaven. It is true that we are obliged to learn from tradition who the writers were of several of the sacred books; but a few facts of this simple nature might securely be trusted to its keeping, though at the same time it would be an improper depository, and an unsafe vehicle for the numerous occurrences, sentiments, and precepts which constitute the christian religion. It is a self-evident proposition, that the chosen companions of Jesus, having witnessed his miracles, having been instructed in his religion, and made intimately acquainted with his character, were qualified in the best manner to convert their experience into history, and to transmit to the latest ages an indubitable standard of christian truth.

Such appear to be our Saviour's motives, as far as we are authorized to judge of them, in nominating his twelve disciples. It becomes a matter of no inconsiderable interest to us, to know something of the history, to ascertain something of the character, of those who were so peculiarly and so highly distinguished.

Who were those, in the first place, whom the Saviour of men, the Prince of Peace, the Son of God, chose out of the whole world, to be his companions, his pupils, his witnesses, his historians, his apostles, his friends? What were their qualities? How were they recommended to the notice of Jesus? What were their occupations, their condition, education, principles? It was a remarkable station which they were called upon to hold; so near the person, so high in the confidence, of the most exalted being who ever appeared on our earth. As disciples ourselves, though it may be unworthy of the name, and as distant from *them* in merit as we are in time, yet as professed disciples of that heavenly Master, we are naturally curious to learn more than simply the names of our favored predecessors. We would make ourselves acquainted with those men who saw, and heard, and touched, and lived and conversed with, that holy prophet of God, for whom we feel a reverence only inferior to that which we entertain toward Him who sent him.

And who were those, we would ask, in the second place, who were appointed by Jesus Christ to publish his religion, and enabled by the assistance of the holy spirit of God to publish it successfully? Who were those, who, in obedience to their Master, went out into all nations, teaching, converting, and baptizing, and planting the parent churches of our faith in learned Greece, and lordly Rome, and benighted Africa, and among those rude people of the north from whom we ourselves are descended? It was no mean work in which they were employed. No revolution of recorded time can equal it in glory; for thrones were subjected to its power, and the poor and humble of the earth were raised by it to an elevation, for which thrones would have been an inadequate substitute. They, like their Lord, were invested with a control over the operations of nature; and more than that, they, like him, and by his authority, and with his instruction, founded an empire the most broad and lasting which has ever existed, over the human mind. Who were they? As Christians, as subjects of that empire, as men amazed, at the same time that we are rejoiced, at what we have heard and what we behold, we are impelled to inquire who they were, who established a dominion which has already covered the civilized world, and is apparently going on with ever encroaching steps, to spread itself over the whole earth? If the lives of any men are interesting, theirs must be peculiarly so. They are the great reformers, the great conquerors, whose empire has been continually increasing and strengthening, while the houses and dynasties of heroes and kings have risen, and flourished, and passed away into forgetfulness and ruin; the only empire which has grown more vigorous and more hopeful with age, because the mind and the heart and the destiny of man, and the good providence of God, are joined to support and perpetuate it. Who were these men?

No elaborate biography, no studied panegyric, has portrayed to us the lives and characters of the apostles of Christ. In their own condensed and simple writings, and in the quite as simple book of their Acts, composed by one of their associates, we must glean such sketches of them as are to be found in connexion with the accounts of their Master and the history of their religion; for of themselves, as individuals, they seldom think of speaking; absorbed in their duty and devoted to their great work, the idea of selfimportance or personal fame never seems to have entered their minds. We shall not, however, esteem them the less, because they were faithful to their calling, and sought not the praise and honor of men, and postponed their own glory to the glory of God. And although our just curiosity may not be gratified by a full and detailed portraiture of these eminent men, who remembered their work, and forgot themselves, yet we shall meet with notices enough in the Scriptures of the New Testament, to enable us to form for ourselves an outline at least of some of their lives and characters. Of some of them we shall find more abundant accounts than of others; for among them, as well as among mankind in general, there was undoubtedly a diversity of power, which caused some of them to stand out in the foreground of action, and others to remain comparatively in shade; though all of them might have been zealous, useful and efficient, and most probably were so.

Though the sacred writings themselves are the only sources of knowledge on this subject, to which we may give implicit credence, yet from other early documents we may obtain some narratives of the latter days of the apostles, which are worthy of a good degree of faith. Making use, therefore, of such authorities as are within my reach, I shall proceed to give some account of the twelve disciples of our Lord; pursuing the order in which they are arranged by Matthew, only because his catalogue is the first which occurs in the common collocation of the Gospel Histories.

SIMON PETER.

Simon, who also received from our Lord the appellation of Peter, is invariably the first named on all the four lists of the apostles, and was, on several accounts, the chief of their company. He was one of the first who was called to be a disciple; though not the very first, for Andrew his brother appears to have been called before him, or at least at the same time with him. He was distinguished above the rest by the solemn predictions and trusts of his Master, by his uncommon zeal, and by his strong natural talents. He is altogether not only a conspicuous disciple, but a remarkable man. The sacred historians give us more copious accounts of him than of the other apostles, and a distinct conception of his character may be gained from what they relate.

He was, as is stated two or three times in the Gospels, the son of John or Jona, who was probably, like his children, a fisherman. The family lived in the town of Bethsaida, on the western side of the lake of

Genesareth, otherwise called the sea of Tiberias, or the sea of Galilee, and consisted, as far as we can ascertain, of Simon himself, his brother, and his father, his wife, and her mother.

As we learn from the evangelist John, Simon was acquainted with Jesus, and had heard him attentively, before he became one of the selected disciples. His brother Andrew was already one of the disciples of John the Baptist, and was standing with a fellow disciple in company with their master, at a time when Jesus was passing by. Looking upon him as he walked, John exclaimed, 'Behold the Lamb of God!' Upon this, the two followed him, and, on the invitation of Jesus, went with him to his dwellingplace and abode with him that day. Convinced of the justice of his claims, Andrew sought for his brother Simon, and saying to him, 'We have found the Messias, or Christ,' he brought him to Jesus. And when Jesus beheld them, he said, 'Thou art Simon, the son of Jona; thou shalt be called Cephas,' which is by interpretation into the Greek, Petra, and into English, a Rock. By this manner of receiving Simon, Jesus manifested that he was acquainted with him, and had formed an estimate of his character; that he had marked him as one who was fitted by his energy and activity to establish his religion on durable foundations; that even now he intended him for a great work. The brothers may at this early period be considered as disciples or pupils of Jesus, though not yet chosen, according to the language of St Mark, to 'be with him always;' for they still continued fishermen.

That event took place a short time after, in the following manner. As Jesus stood by the lake, surrounded by a crowd who were pressing upon him to hear the word of God, he saw Simon and Andrew, in the practice of their usual occupation, and washing their nets on the shore. He entered their vessel, and prayed them to thrust out a little from the land, that he might the more conveniently teach the people. Then, having finished his discourse, he bade them launch out into the deep, and let down their net for a draught of fishes. It is now that we begin to perceive the ardent, affectionate, and confiding character of Peter. Though he and his companions had been toiling through the night without the least success, yet he at once consented to make another effort, in obedience to the wishes of Jesus. 'Nevertheless, at thy word,' he says, 'I will let down the net.' This was no sooner done, than such a multitude of fishes were enclosed, that the net began to break, and they were obliged to call their partners, who were in another ship, to assist them, and both ships were so filled with what they drew in as to be near sinking. On beholding this, Simon Peter, ever a man of impulses, 'fell down at Jesus' knees, saying, Depart from me, for I am a sinful man, O Lord.' In a transport of fearful humility he beseeches Jesus to leave him, and not to stay with one so unworthy of his holy and wonderful presence. But Jesus, instead of leaving him, now gives him the call to his apostleship, saying to him, 'Fear not; from henceforth thou shalt catch men;' or as the other evangelists write, applying the words to both the brethren,

'I will make you fishers of men.' Readily accepting the invitation to become the constant companions of the Messiah, and perhaps secretly expecting worldly advantage from their connexion with so great a personage, they straightway left all, their property, their home, and their former friends, and followed him.

Peter's character now rapidly unfolds itself; a character of strong and contrasted features; bold, honest, and vehement, and yet wavering and inconstant; now forward and daring before all his companions, and now more timid than any of them. Wherever we meet with him, it is the same Simon that we see; distinguished alike for high and generous virtues, and for faults inconsistent with those virtues and altogether unworthy of them. Strength and weakness, courage and irresolution, impetuosity and indecision, are mixed up in his temperament in a striking and yet perfectly natural combination; and at the bottom of the whole, there is a purity of feeling, and an integrity of purpose, which endear him to his Master, and fit him at last for his important destination and office.

One of the occasions which may be noticed as developing these characteristics, is that of his attempt to walk on the sea to meet Jesus. We are informed that after the miracle of the loaves and fishes, which took place on one side of the lake, Jesus commanded his disciples to pass over to the other in a vessel, while he remained to send the multitude away. A storm overtook the ship when she was in the midst of the sea, and, while she was tossing on the waves, Jesus came to them in the fourth watch of the night, or towards morning, walking on the sea, as on dry land. At this extraordinary sight, the disciples were troubled, saying 'It is a spirit;' and to such a height was their terror excited, that they cried out for fear. But Jesus immediately spoke to them, and bade them not to be afraid, for it was himself. No sooner does Peter hear his voice, than he not only dismisses his fear, but gives loose to his enthusiasm, and unwilling to wait till his Master reaches the vessel, and perhaps too, tempted a little to display his faith, and do some great thing, he exclaims, before the others have recovered the use of their speech, 'Lord, if it be thou, bid me come unto thee on the water.' And Jesus, knowing him perfectly, and willing at once to gratify, to test, and to instruct him, said, 'Come.' Peter descends from the ship, and walks towards his Master. But the storm was stronger than his trust; and when he felt himself out, so strangely and awfully, amidst the dashing foam and the boisterous wind, he was afraid, and he forgot his confidence; and his faith, which hitherto had borne him up, grew faint and unable to hold him, and beginning to sink, he cried again, and with the voice of despair, to Jesus, 'Lord, save me!' 'And immediately Jesus stretched forth his hand, and caught him, and said unto him, O thou of little faith, wherefore didst thou doubt?' That was all the Saviour said; that mild rebuke, so unlike the denunciations which his professed followers in other ages have launched at what they have been pleased to call, but could not with certainty know to be, deficiencies of faith; that mild rebuke from him who did know all things, was the only punishment for the failing faith of the disciple; 'Wherefore didst thou doubt?' Wherefore, after seeing what thou hast seen, and hearing what thou hast heard, couldst thou doubt? And he raised the selfconvicted man, and brought him into the ship, and 'the wind ceased.'

Notwithstanding Simon's occasional misgivings and temporary weaknesses, his fidelity was in the main firm and certain, because it was founded on the real goodness and tenderness of his nature. There was a time, when, as related in the sixth chapter of the Gospel of John, many of the followers of Jesus 'went back, and walked no more with him,' because he spoke to them obscurely and figuratively of his office and kingdom, and because, from what they did understand, they began to suspect that there was something much more spiritual, and much less lucrative and splendid in his proposed dominion, than suited with their earthly conceptions. They went back, therefore, and walked no more with him. Then said Jesus unto the twelve, his chosen twelve, 'Will ye also go away?' To whose heart, of those twelve hearts, does the affecting appeal first find its way? Who answers it first? The same man who but just now was afraid of the wind. 'Then Simon Peter answered him, Lord, to whom shall we go? thou hast the words of eternal life. And we believe and are sure that thou art that Christ, the Son of the living God.' Generous, fullhearted, though too inconstant disciple! Though others desert that good and gentle Master, thou wilt not leave him. In this time of trial, thy heart has kept thee right. Thou art like some tall and comely tree, whose pliant trunk is swayed hither and thither by the passing storm, but whose tenacious root spreads wide abroad, and pierces deep beneath, and still reclaims the waving plant, and binds it firmly to the soil it loves.

At yet another time also, Peter made the same open and bold confession. It was when Jesus, having asked his disciples, whom men said that he was, and having received their answer, put the question to them, saying, 'But whom say ye that I am?' Again it is the ardent Simon who advances before the rest, and answers unhesitatingly, 'Thou art the Christ, the Son of the living God.' This renewed proof of his attachment and faith draws forth the marked approbation of his Master, who answered him and said, 'Blessed art thou, Simon, son of Jona; for flesh and blood hath not revealed it unto thee, but my Father who is in heaven. The spirit of God, himself, hath enlightened thee. And I say also unto thee, that thou art Peter. I have already called thee a rock, and upon this rock will I build my church, and the gates of the place of death shall not prevail against it. Upon thy exertions shall the foundations of my church be laid, and laid so strongly that they shall never be overturned nor destroyed. And I will give unto thee the keys of the kingdom of heaven; and whatsoever thou shalt bind on earth shall be bound in heaven; and whatsoever thou shalt loose on earth, shall be loosed in heaven.'

That by these words of Jesus a certain degree of apostolic preeminence was conferred on Peter, I think is too plain to be disputed; though some overzealous Protestants have denied the fact. But why they should wish to deny it, I cannot see; for I cannot see how the primacy which his Lord chose to confer on him should disturb them, nor can I see, on the other hand, how that primacy, being fully admitted, can be an argument for the papal supremacy. If Peter was thought by his master worthy of standing first among his disciples, who shall say that he did not deserve the dignity? But what was the nature of that dignity? 'On this rock will I build my church,' said Jesus. The christian church was not built on Peter alone, nor by him alone; for all the apostles contributed to the edifice; but to Peter was commissioned the duty of first declaring the gospel to the Jews, and indeed, by a special vision, to the Gentiles also; and the centurion and his family, converted and baptized by him, were the firsts fruits of Christianity out of the Jewish pale. He was therefore the foundation of the church; the rock on which its beginnings were laid. But there is nothing transferable in this part of his dignity, at least. The foundations of the church are not to be laid twice and thrice, and over and over again, because a series of men calling themselves popes, claim to be his successors. Neither is there any promise of transmitting the keys of the kingdom of heaven, which signify only that authority which Peter, as an accredited apostle of Christ was to have in his ministry. He was empowered to act in general as an ambassador from Heaven; to enact regulations, to establish and to break down, to do and to undo, with the concurrence and power of the Head of the Church himself. And this authority, let it be remembered, was committed to all the rest of the apostles in precisely the same words; for they also were to preach their Master's doctrine to the world, and needed his delegated power in things pertaining to his kingdom. To them also did he say, therefore, 'Whatsoever ye shall bind on earth, shall be bound in heaven; and whatsoever ye shall loose on earth, shall be loosed in heaven.' The preeminence of Peter, then, appears to be simply a precedence among his brethren and equals, which was conceded to his abilities and energy; and a preference which was bestowed on him as a teacher of the religion of Christ. But there is no promise, no intimation, in the scriptures, that even this preeminence was to descend on other men; nor does the similarity between the popes of Rome and Simon Peter of Bethsaida, between the triple crowned sovereigns of Christendom, who once set their feet on kings' necks, and the plain fisherman of the sea of Galilee, seem to be, in any point of view, very close or striking.

Whatever elation of heart may have been produced in Peter by the praise of a beloved Master, it was almost immediately doomed to be checked and mortified by the same impartial voice; for in the very chapter which records this last occurrence, we are told that the disciple drew upon himself one of the severest rebukes which Jesus ever uttered. 'From that time forth,' says the evangelist, 'began Jesus to show unto his disciples, how that he must go unto Jerusalem, and suffer many things of the elders and chief priests and scribes, and be killed, and be raised again the third day.' Intimations of this kind were always peculiarly unwelcome and enigmatical to the disciples; and on this occasion Peter comes forward as usual, and with even more than his usual warmth, took up his Master, and began to rebuke him, saying, 'Be it far from thee, Lord; this shall not be unto thee.' Though he had so lately acknowledged Jesus to be the Messiah, and had adhered to him in his humble and unkingly condition, yet even he had not wholly disjoined the ideas of worldly power and dignity from the person and office of the expected Saviour; and the thought of his violent and shameful death was altogether shocking to him. But Jesus was particularly anxious to crush these misapprehensions, and to familiarize his followers to his real situation and his approaching and inevitable fate. He therefore thought proper, before them all, to express in a manner which might make them feel, how earnest his disapprobation was of their temporal expectations and fancies. 'He turned, and said unto Peter, get thee behind me, Satan; [tempter, adversary;] thou art an offence unto me; for thou savourest not the things that be of God, but those that be of men.' The disciples had yet to learn, Simon Peter had yet to learn, how pure, unearthly and immortal that religion was, which they were appointed one day to promulgate; how it associated itself more with human suffering than with human glory and pride; more with the secret sympathies and internal affections, much more, than with the outward adornments of our nature; and the early death of their Master—an event which they could not bear to think, and could hardly conceive of, but which he, the divine Master, saw with a clear and steady vision—was yet to teach them, that the infant doctrine which was to go through the world, consoling the sorrows of the mourner, and pouring balm into wounded bosoms, was itself first to be nurtured with tears, and baptized in blood.

There is no doubt that Peter received his Master's rebuke properly, for we find that he was still distinguished and confided in by him. He, together with James and John, was selected to witness the transfiguration on the mount; and in the same company, he had also witnessed the resurrection of the daughter of Jairus. It appears moreover, that about this time he and his Lord dwelt together at Capernaum, in the same house; for when the gatherers of the annual tribute came to Peter, he went into the house, and was there told by Jesus how he was to obtain a piece of money which would pay for them both. It would appear, therefore, that they lived together, and if so, that the disciple was high in the favor and confidence of his Master. He seems also to have exercised a sort of conceded preeminence among the twelve, as we often find him speaking in their name and behalf, both in asking and in answering questions. His rank is now evidently fixed. He is honored by his Master, notwithstanding his imperfections, and he is the head of the apostles, both from appointment and character.

But his fault of impetuosity is not yet mended. It is one of the last faults, perhaps, which ever is mended, because it is constitutional. On that most solemn night of the last supper, Jesus, in order that he might at once testify his affection for his disciples, whom he loved unto the end, and show them also an example of practical humility, began to wash their feet, as if he had been their servant. When he came to Peter, that disciple, hurt and grieved that his Master should undertake so menial an office, gives way to his feelings, again presumes to dictate to that very Master, and exclaims, 'Lord, dost thou wash my feet?' Jesus condescends to expostulate with him, and to assure him that he would soon explain to him the act which now appeared so strange. 'What I do, thou knowest not now, but thou shalt know hereafter.' But Peter will not yield, nor listen, but answers, 'Thou shalt never wash my feet.' To which Jesus replies, 'If I wash thee not, thou hast no part with me.' That is, 'If you will not receive this symbolical lesson of humility; if you cannot cease your disputes about who shall be greatest in my kingdom; if you will not divest yourselves of your notions of place and dignity, and become lowly, meek, and mutually kind, as my disciples ought to be, and must be, if they desire my approbation, then I must discard you from my service, and deprive you of my friendship.' Peter, subdued at the bare intimation of forfeiting his Master's esteem, and again driven beyond the just limits of duty by the sudden revulsion of his ungoverned feelings, cries out, 'Lord, not my feet only, but my hands and my head. Wash me all over, if it be thy will, only take not from me thy love.' How perfectly natural is the whole of this scene; how consistent with the previous character of Peter; how just to the character of his Lord!

And now the time draws near, when the first of the apostles is to be tried more severely, and to fall more sadly than ever. Soon after Jesus had washed his disciples' feet, he began to talk to them, in a most affecting strain, of his speedy death and his return to his Father. Peter's feelings are again alarmed, and he declares that wherever his Master may go, he will follow him, and go with him, even into prison and to death. 'Though all men shall be offended because of thee, yet I will never be offended; I will lay down my life for thy sake.' Jesus, better aware of his disciple's weakness, and knowing that it would not be equal to the approaching trial, mournfully answered, 'Wilt thou lay down thy life for my sake? Verily, verily, I say unto thee, the cock shall not crow, till thou hast denied me thrice.' And yet the ardent disciple spoke the more vehemently, and said, 'Though I should die with thee, yet will I not deny thee.'

Let us mark the result. After discoursing to his disciples, in those beautiful words which are to be found in the fourteenth, fifteenth and sixteenth chapters of the Gospel of John, Jesus went out with them, and coming to a place which was named Gethsemane, left them there, and taking with him Peter, James and John, to watch with him, withdrew apart to pray to his Father. When he returned to these favored three, he found them, not watching, but asleep. It was towards morning; and with frames oppressed with fatigue, and minds made heavy with sorrow, they had not been able to watch with their suffering and agonized Lord during his short absence, but had sunk down in a leaden slumber. More in pity than in wrath, the Saviour, addressing himself particularly to Peter, as the individual who had boasted the loudest, and had the most need of warning, said to him, 'What! could ye not watch with me one hour? After all your professions, can you not banish sleep, and prove your attachment, by a vigil, for my sake, of one short hour? Watch and pray, that ye enter not into temptation; the spirit indeed is full of courage, but the flesh is weak.' Again and again he returns to them, and still finds them sleeping. Then comes the traitor Judas, with his band, and they are roused effectually; and Peter, who could not watch for his Master at his earnest request, undertakes, without his authority, to fight for him; and he drew his sword, and smote a servant of the high priest, and cut off his ear. So much easier is it to fight, than to be dutiful; and so much the more readily could Peter obey the impulses of his passions, than the behest of his Lord. Jesus calmly reproves the offender, and then all his disciples forsook him and fled.

There were two, however, who did not wholly forsake him; but still, though at a distance, followed him. One of these two was Peter; he sincerely loved his Master, and though just rebuked by him, he resolves not to lose sight of him, but follows him afar off, even into the court of the high priest's house. There, trembling, anxious, and vibrating between fear and affection, he takes his seat with the servants at the fire. He does not remain there long unsuspected, but is charged with being one of the followers of Jesus. His fear preponderates; his bold resolution, so lately formed, gives way; he denies all knowledge of his Master. Yes, Simon Peter, the leader of the twelve, the rock of the church, the confidant of Jesus, who walked on the sea, who held the spiritual keys, who saw the dead raised up, who witnessed the glorious transfiguration, who declared himself but just now ready to be bound, and led to death for his Master, now sits among menials, denying him to menials! with the mingled flush of dread and shame upon his cheek, denying to a set of scoffing hirelings of a corrupt palace, that he ever knew that kind and trusting Master, whom he had so lately acknowledged to be the princely Messiah, the Son of the King of Heaven! By and by, and from another quarter, he is again attacked with the same charge; 'Thou also wast with Jesus of Nazareth.' Having committed himself once, and not having recovered from his confusion and fear; detected, and yet obstinate; struggling between contrition and wrath, a deep sense of humiliation, and a strong dread of exposure, he again 'denied before them all, saying, I know not what thou sayest.' Only imagine the scene! Jesus, standing bound, as if he had been a criminal, surrounded by soldiers and exulting enemies, and questioned like an apprehended culprit by the high priest, but dignified, collected, and prepared for the worst; while just below is his chief disciple, in the midst of a servile crowd, agonized with terror, and endeavouring with all his native vehemence, and with a native accent too, which of itself contradicts him, to clear himself be-

c

fore his contemptible accusers from the imputation of having any thing to do with one whom he had been following daily and hourly for months, and whom, but a few moments ago, he had promised to follow to prison and to death! But the measure of his degradation is not yet full; for again, the third time, is the charge repeated; 'Surely, thou also art one of them, for thy speech betrayeth thee.' And then, as others are apt to do, who become more boisterous the more they are in the wrong and the nearer they are to detection, and who call the God of truth to witness their transgressions of truth, the unhappy man 'began to curse and to swear, saying, I know not the man. And immediately the cock crew.' How dark is the account now of disgrace and crime against the fallen disciple! Ingratitude, cowardice, falsehood, profanity! It was the lowest fall; and, thank God, it was the last. 'The Lord turned, and looked upon Peter.' What a volume of pathos and eloquence is contained in those few simple words! His Lord looked upon him, 'and with that gracious and chiding look called him back to himself and him.' He remembered all; remembered his Master's love, remembered his Master's warning, remembered his own duty. Conviction falls upon him, repentance overwhelms him, and he went out and wept bitterly.

From this time till after the crucifixion of Jesus, we hear no more of Peter. He probably passed this distressing interval in remorse and tears; and there is no doubt that his repentance was entire and sincere, and that his character was much improved and purified by the late fiery trial through which it had been led; for we find that Jesus, on the morning of his resurrection, after he had shown himself to Mary Magdalene, appeared also to Peter, in testimony of his continued confidence in him; and that Peter had returned to his allegiance is manifest from the fact that he was the first of the male disciples who descended into the tomb wherein the Saviour had been laid.

Some days afterwards, as several of the disciples were fishing together in a vessel, on the sea of Tiberias, Jesus appeared to them on the shore. On this occasion we may again observe a symptom of Peter's characteristic ardor. No sooner had he understood from John that it was the Lord who stood on the shore, and had been speaking with them, than he girt his fisher's coat about him, cast himself into the sea, and in this manner gained the land, while the rest came after him in the vessel. When they had all dined on the fish which had been taken, Jesus required of Peter that thrice repeated assurance of his love, in which a fanciful interpreter would discover a direct allusion to the late thrice repeated denial. On receiving each assurance, his Lord gives him an especial charge to feed his sheep. He then signified to him, though darkly, by what death he should glorify God; but refused to gratify his curiosity respecting the fate of his fellow disciple, John.

In the Gospels, we have no further information respecting this apostle. On turning to the book of Acts, however, he is immediately presented to us in his former rank and station, as chief of the apostles, speaking in their name, and presiding at their meetings. It is he who proposes that the vacated place of Judas Iscariot should be supplied by lot. When some of those who were present at the effusion of the Holy Spirit, and the gift of tongues, mocked at the disciples, and said that they were full of new wine, it was Peter who in a most spirited manner refuted the slander, and spoke so powerfully of his Master's claims, that on the same day there were added to the number of christian believers, about three thousand souls. It was Peter who healed the lame man at the Beautiful Gate of the temple; who addressed the people on that occasion; who, when arraigned before the chief priests, declared so boldly to them that salvation was alone by Jesus Christ; and who, when he and his companion John were commanded not to speak at all nor teach in that name, returned, jointly with the beloved disciple, that heroic answer, 'Whether it be right in the sight of God, to hearken unto you more than unto God, judge ye.' It was Peter who exposed the deception of Ananias and his wife Sapphira, and at whose feet they both fell down dead. And it was Peter, who by his shadow alone, healed many who were laid in his way.

After Samaria had, through the instrumentality of Philip, received the word of God, Peter and John were sent there by the apostles, in order that they might lay their hands on the converts, and cause them to receive the Holy Spirit. And then it was that Peter so indignantly rebuked Simon the sorcerer, who thought that the gift of God might be purchased with money. 'Thy money perish with thee,' said he; 'thou hast neither part nor lot in this matter, for thy heart is not right in the sight of God.'

We now find him very actively engaged in the duties of his apostleship, 'passing throughout all quarters,' performing miracles, preaching the word, and feeding the sheep of the great shepherd. At Lydda, he healed a certain man named Æneas, who had been sick with the palsy eight years; and at the neighbouring town of Joppa he raised to life a pious female disciple by the name of Tabitha, or Dorcas.

At Joppa he abode many days with one Simon, a tanner. It was while he was living here, that he was called to instruct and baptize Cornelius, the centurion, who dwelt in Cæsarea; to prepare him for which duty, he was taught, in a remarkable vision, not to call any creature of God common or unclean, and that God is no respecter of persons, but in every nation he that feareth him, and worketh righteousness, is accepted with him. With these convictions on his mind, he obeys the call of Cornelius to come to him, and while he is addressing him, witnesses the descent of the spirit on him and his family, and orders them to be baptized in the name of the Lord. Thus he fulfilled to the utmost the prediction with which his name of Peter was conferred on him, and founded the christian church in both the Jewish and the Gentile world. It was an event of which we at this period can hardly estimate the importance. Devoid of Jewish prejudices and antipathies, we can hardly conceive with what consternation the Jewish converts, who, as Jews, had

c*

always cherished the belief that religion and truth and God's peculiar favor always had been, and always were to be, confined to them, must have listened to the intelligence, that the chief of the apostles had been breaking down the wall, and drawing up the veil which were interposed between the faithful people and the rest of the world, and that henceforth there was to be no spiritual distinction between Hebrew and Greek, Jew and Gentile. Some conception of this indignant surprise of theirs may be formed from the recorded circumstance, that when Peter had returned to Jerusalem, 'they that were of the circumcision,' including his fellow apostles, and indeed the whole christian church, 'contended with him, saying, thou wentest in to men uncircumcised, and didst eat with them.' It was enough to provoke their amazement that he simply eat with them. But Peter had the stedfastness to defend himself, and expound the whole matter to them from the beginning; and so much were they impressed by the force and reason of his words, that they acquiesced in peace, 'and glorified God, saying, Then hath God also to the Gentiles granted repentance unto life.'

Not long after this, Peter was put into prison by Herod, but was set free by an angel. He then went down from Judea to Cæsarea, and there abode; very probably in the house, or under the protection of Cornelius, his distinguished convert.

The next time that we hear of him, is at the meeting of apostles and elders, which is generally called the Council of Jerusalem, and which was convened to settle the long and vehemently agitated question, again brought up by some of the believing Pharisees, whether it was needful to circumcise all converts, and command them to keep the law of Moses. When there had been much disputing, Peter rose up, and gave his decided opinion against the necessity of circumcising the Gentiles, or bringing them under the ceremonial law. And with this opinion the Council at last coincided.

With the history of this Council, the notices of Peter's life in the Acts of the apostles come to an end. He is named a few times in the epistles of Paul, and once with reprehension. That apostle tells us, in his epistle to the Galatians, that when Peter was come to Antioch, he withstood him to the face, because he was to be blamed; for that although he had already eaten with Gentiles, according to his own new principles so openly professed, yet when some of the circumcision came to Antioch, he withdrew from the Gentiles, from fear of the circumcised. This was an inconsistency, certainly, and shows that some remains of weakness still lingered about the character of Peter; but it is the only inconsistency which is laid to his charge from the time of his Master's resurrection; and he can easily be forgiven, when we consider how much he had done and suffered, ever since that event, in his Master's name, and for his Master's cause.

All that remains to be said of this remarkable man, is to be gathered, not from the scriptures, but from other early accounts, the authority of which, though not to be compared with that of the scriptures, should be held in a due degree of respect. We are informed by Eusebius, that Origen wrote of him, that 'he was supposed to have preached to the Jews of the dispersion in Pontus, Galatia, Bithynia, Cappadocia, and Asia. And at length coming to Rome, was crucified with his head downwards.' This kind of death he was said to have requested, out of a feeling of humble respect to his Master. If so, it is an affecting conclusion of his eventful life, and another striking exhibition of his ardent character. He conceived it too great an honor that such an one as he should meet his death erect, and looking upwards, like his beloved and venerated Lord; and so, with his head in the dust, he closed his labors, his failings, his sufferings, and his life.

He is said to have been bishop of Rome for twentyfour or twentyfive years, and to have died at about the age of seventyfive. We are also told, that he was first buried in the catacombs, two miles from the city, and afterwards deposited in the Vatican; and it is the belief of the Roman Catholics that his body now reposes under the splendid church which is called by his name.

It is probable that he was a married man, and that his wife accompanied him in his journies. St Paul is thought to intimate as much, when he says, in his first epistle to the Corinthians,* 'Have we not power to lead about a sister, a wife, as well as other apostles, and as the brethren of the Lord, and Cephas?'

Two epistles of Peter are received into the Canon of the New Testament. The authenticity of the first is well established and generally allowed. It is addressed 'to the strangers scattered throughout Pontus,

* Chap. ix. 5.

Galatia, Cappadocia, Asia, and Bithynia.' By these 'strangers' is most probably meant the Jewish Christians who sojourned in those regions; though some commentators would have the term to apply both to Jewish and Gentile converts. The epistle was written from Rome, which is figuratively denominated Babylon, in the concluding salutation. Its purpose was to strengthen and comfort those to whom it was addressed, who were suffering under the persecutions which had begun to be fiercely waged against them by the heathens. The topics urged in it, are equal to its design, and are highly consolatory and animating. Of the whole epistle, Erasmus says, 'It is worthy of the Prince of the Apostles, and full of apostolical dignity and authority. It is sparing in words, but full of sense.'

The genuineness of the second epistle has been called in question, from early times. It never was fully disproved, however, and there was good reason for numbering it at last among the sacred books. The testimony of Eusebius concerning it is as follows: 'One epistle of Peter, called his first, is acknowledged. This the presbyters of ancient times have quoted in their writings, as undoubtedly genuine. But that called his second, we have been informed by tradition, has not been received as a part of the New Testament. Nevertheless, appearing to many to be useful, it hath been carefully studied with the other scriptures.' Origen, who flourished in the third century, says of the two epistles, 'Peter, on whom the church is built, hath left an epistle universally acknowledged. Let it be granted that he has also wrote a second; for it is doubted.' That it was doubted, is no proof of any thing more than that the evidence in its favor was not so complete as that which could be produced for other sacred books. And it may be said, both of this epistle and the few other writings of the canon which were not fully received, that they manifest in their history, how careful the first Christians were in examining the claims of alleged apostolical compositions, and adopting them as of authority in the church. The learned and candid Lardner observes, that so well founded was the judgment of those early Christians, concerning the books of the New Testament, that no writing which was by them pronounced genuine, has, since their time, been found spurious; neither have we, at this day, the least reason to think any book genuine, which they rejected.

We may be authorized, therefore, in accepting the second epistle of Peter as his true work, notwithstanding the rather doubtful character of its evidence. If it was written by him, it was probably written to the same persons, and from the same place with the first. It was written, also, not long after the first, and not long before the death of the apostle.

ANDREW.

Of Andrew, the brother of Simon Peter, we are told but little in the sacred writings; not enough, indeed, to enable us to form any estimate of his character. We may be permitted to conjecture, however, from the circumstance of his having been a disciple of John the Baptist, and also from his having gone voluntarily to hear the instructions of Jesus, and thus made himself his first disciple among those who were afterwards his apostles; we may conjecture, I say, from these circumstances, which have already been stated in the life of Peter, that the temperament of Andrew was sober and religious, and that his mind was remarkably open to the reception of truth. So far as we can argue at all, we may argue the existence of every thing that is good, from such commendable appearances. We can easily believe that he was a serious, candid, stedfast man; very probably without the shining talents and the burning zeal of his brother, and quite as probably without his brother's prominent faults. That not much is recorded of him, is a proof that he was not very forward or active among the twelve; but it is by no means a proof that he wanted good sense, discretion, or stability.

We find, concerning him, that he was the disciple, who, just before the miracle of feeding the five thousand, informed Jesus that there was a lad present who had five barley loaves and two small fishes, and then added the question, 'But what are they among so many?' This question, on the first view of it, seems to denote that Andrew had no idea that it was practicable to feed the multitude, and merely mentioned the small quantity of provisions in despair, and as an aggravation of their condition; but it is possible too that he may have entertained a secret hope that it was in his Master's power to relieve their wants even with the five loaves and two fishes, and that he propounded the question in a hesitating manner, that he might draw forth his Master's intentions. If this last is the fact, it shows that he possessed more faith than was often manifested by the other disciples, though not such an enthusiastic faith as was sometimes displayed by his more ardent brother.

We read also of Andrew, that when certain Greeks, who had come up to Jerusalem to worship at the feast of the Passover, expressed to Philip their desire to see Jesus, Philip mentioned the request to Andrew, and then they went both together to impart it to Jesus. These Greeks were no doubt what were called Proselytes of the Gate, or Greeks who had been converted to the acknowledgment and worship of the true God; but who, on account of their Gentile extraction, were not entitled to all the religious privileges and distinctions of native Jews. They had heard of the fame of Jesus, and desired to be introduced to his presence, not only to gratify their curiosity, but, if we may judge from the succeeding discourse of our Saviour, to inquire concerning his kingdom. The precaution which was used by Philip in preferring their request, is a sign, in the first place, that he was doubtful whether a Gentile ought to be brought into the company of the Messiah; and secondly, that Andrew was, in his opinion, a person with whom he might profitably consult, in an affair which appeared to him to be of some moment and delicacy.

It was a few days after this, that Andrew, together with Peter, James and John, asked Jesus, privately, what the sign should be, when all the things, which he had just been telling them respecting the destruction of the temple, should be fulfilled. This is all which is related of this apostle in the Gospels. In no other part of the writings of the New Testament is he ever mentioned, excepting as he is included in the mention of the apostles as a body.

Other ancient accounts inform us, that he preached the gospel in various countries, and was at last crucified at Patræ in Achaia, by order of Egæus, proconsul of that province. His body was afterwards removed to Constantinople, and he is considered by the modern Greeks, as founder of the Byzantine or Constantinopolitan church.

JAMES THE GREATER.

JAMES, the son of Zebedee, and the brother of John, is the third named on Matthew's list of the apostles. Of his father we are told nothing; but his mother, as appears by a comparison of parallel passages, was Salome, who emulated her children in attachment to the Saviour, and is spoken of as one of those women who followed and occasionally served him, who accompanied him to the cross, and were the first who were permitted to see him after his resurrection. This James has received the surname of the Greater, or Elder, to distinguish him from the other apostle, James the Less, of whom I shall speak hereafter.

He, with his brother John, pursued the same occupation with their townsmen Peter and Andrew, and were partners with them. They were also washing their nets on the shore, when Jesus entered the vessel of their partners. They beheld the miraculous draught of fishes; they assisted to secure it; they were astonished at it, and when Jesus, after calling

Peter and Andrew, called them also, 'they immediately left the ship and their father, and followed him.'

Here I cannot help requesting my readers to pause a moment, and consider the fortunes, the singular, and, if the word were holy enough, I would say romantic, fortunes of these four men. Simon and Andrew, James and John, brethren of two different families, dwell together with their parents, in a village at the northern extremity of a lake or small sea, in the district of Galilee, and on the confines of the land of Judea. The sea is a large sea to them, and to them the towns, which here and there dot its coast, and the light barks, which, for the purposes of amusement, or traffic, or their own calling, skim along its pleasant waters, are the world. They are fishermen. Day by day do they rise up to the contented exercise of their toil, to throw their nets, to spread their sails, to ply their oars, and, when successful in pursuit, to dispose of their freight in their native village, or the neighbouring towns, for the support of themselves and their families. They are friends; they have joined themselves to each other in their humble profession, and agreed to share profit and loss, storm and calm, together. Their low roofed dwellings look out on each other, and on their native lake, and within these dwellings are bosoms which throb anxiously at their protracted absence, and beat gladly at their return. Their boats contain all their wealth, and their cottages all that they love. Their fathers, perhaps their ancestors, were fishers before them. They themselves have no idea of a different lot. The only changes on which they calculate, are the changes of the weather and the vicissitudes of their calling; and the only great interruptions of the even courses of their lives, to which they look forward, are the annual journies which they take, at the periods of solemn festival, to the great city of Jerusalem. Thus they live, and thus they expect to live, till they lie down to sleep with their fathers, as calmly, as unknowing, and as unknown as they.

Look at them, on the shore of their lake. Think not of them as apostles, as holy men; but look at them as they actually were on the morning when you first hear of them from the historian. They have been toiling through a weary night, and have caught nothing; and now, somewhat disheartened at their ill success, they are engaged in spreading their nets, washing them, and preparing them, as they hope, for a more fortunate expedition. Presently, surrounded by an eager crowd, that teacher approaches, whom they have before seen, and whose instructions some of them have already listened to. With his demeanour of quiet but irresistible dignity, he draws toward the spot where they are employed; he enters Simon's vessel, and prays him to thrust out a little distance from the land; then he speaks to that assembled multitude as never man spake; then he bids Simon launch out further, and cast his net in the deep; then follows the overwhelming draught of fishes; and then those four partners, filled with wonder and awe, are called to quit their boats, and throw by their nets, and become fishers of men.

And now what a change, like the change of a dream

or of enchantment, has passed over their lives, dividing what was, from what was to be! It was long before they themselves were aware, how entire and how stupendous it was. In a few years, they are to be the principal actors in the most extraordinary events of recorded time. Home, kindred, country, are to be forsaken forever. Their nets may hang and bleach in the sun; their boats may rot piecemeal on the shore; for the owners of them are far away, sailing over seas to which that of Gennesareth is a pond; exciting whole cities and countries to wonder and tumult; answering before kings; imprisoned, persecuted, tortured; their whole existence a storm, and a greater one than ever swept over their lake. On the peaceful shore of that lake, even their bones may not rest. Their ashes are to be separated from the ashes of their kindred. Their blood is to be sprinkled on foreign soils; the headsman and executioner are to preside over their untimely obsequies. A few years more, and the fame and the doctrine of these fishermen have gone out into all lands. Magnificent churches are called by their names. Kingdoms adopt them for their tutelar saints; and the men who claim to succeed to the office of one of them, rule for centuries over all civilized kingdoms with a despotic and overshadowing sway, and by virtue of that claim give away a continent, a world, which, when their predecessor lived, was entirely unknown. History tells us of a fisherman of Sicily, who was raised to that island's throne; but who will compare that, or any earthly throne, to the twelve thrones which were set up over the twelve tribes of Israel? What is a king of Sicily to an apostle of Christ? A wonderful man has risen up in our own, as we call it, wonderful time, risen up from a moderate station to the empire of Europe; and yet the eight volumes which another wonderful man has written of that emperor's deeds and fortunes, have not preserved, and cannot preserve, such a name for his hero, as is secured by hardly more than eight lines, which tell us of those men who first fished for their living on the sea of Galilee, and then were called to be the apostles of Christ.

My digression has led me far away, over distant countries and through many years. Let us return to the land of Judea, and the history of James. We ascertain, that among the twelve, he was one of those who were the most honored by the confidence of Jesus. With his former partner Simon, and his brother John, he was selected, as we have already seen, to accompany his Lord on several very important occasions; such as that of the resurrection of Jairus' daughter, the transfiguration, and the agony in the garden. It was perhaps on the strength of this manifest confidence, and of her own services, that Salome, the mother of James and John, made that ambitious and truly maternal request to Jesus, that her sons might sit on his right and left hand in his kingdom; that is, enjoy the two highest dignities next to his own, when he, as the Messiah, should mount the throne of Israel.

This is another instance of the universal misapprehension which then prevailed, and from which the disciples of Jesus were not free, concerning the office of the expected Messiah. It was with a complete understanding of this misapprehension, that Jesus now answered the deceived and partial mother; 'Ye know not what ye ask. Are ye able to drink of the cup that I shall drink of, and to be baptized with the baptism that I am baptized with? Will you partake wholly of my lot; will you be able to adhere to me through every adversity, and share all my toils and dangers with me?' The brothers, whom in reality Jesus addressed, and through whose instigation it was that their mother had spoken to him, now answered him, under the persuasion that they could readily undergo a few trials in his service, in order to be at length advanced to great dignity under him, 'We are able.' How full of melancholy meaning is the reply of our Saviour. 'Ye shall drink indeed of my cup, ye shall drain its full measure of sufferings to the dregs; and be baptized with the baptism that I am baptized with, even the waters of violent death; but to sit on my right hand and on my left, to prescribe your rank and degree in this world or the next, is not mine to give; it shall be given to those for whom it is prepared of my Father.' As soon as the other disciples heard of the ambitious application of the sons of Zebedee, they were moved with indignation against them; but their Master, to quell their rising jealousy and ill will, told them that the princes of the Gentiles, merely temporal governors, did indeed exercise that authority which they were so anxious to possess; but that it should not be so among them, but that he who would be great, truly great, among them, should minister the most kindly to each other's wishes and necessities; for in his kingdom that man would be chief in estimation and place, who was chief in benevolence, usefulness, and virtue.

The brothers are again exhibited to us in no very amiable light. We read in the ninth chapter of the Gospel of Luke, that when the time approached in which Jesus was to finish his mission on earth, he set out to go from Galilee to Jerusalem; and as his way led through Samaria, he sent messengers before him to a Samaritan village, to prepare for his hospitable reception. The Samaritans, knowing that he was going up to the feast of the Passover, and piqued that he should pass by their own temple, which was the rival of that of Jerusalem, would not receive him. The anger of James and John was kindled by this rudeness, and they said to Jesus, 'Lord, wilt thou that we command fire to come down from heaven, and consume them, even as Elias did? But he turned and rebuked them, and said, Ye know not what manner of spirit ye are of. For the Son of man is not come to destroy men's lives, but to save them.' The evangelist adds, in words simply descriptive of our Saviour's gentleness and forbearance, 'And they went to another village.'

We may collect from these notices, that James was disposed to be ambitious and passionate; somewhat resembling Peter in these respects, as also in his real attachment to his Master. We can with difficulty suppose that his brother John heartily joined him on the abovementioned occasions, because his character, as we shall see hereafter, was of a very gentle order; and therefore it is probable that he was prevailed upon by the more vehement and energetic James to concur in his sentiments and projects at those times. It can hardly be regretted, however, that these exposures of human infirmity took place, when we advert to the excellent precepts on the subjects of ambition and revenge which they drew forth from the Saviour. And it is likewise to be observed, that with all his gentleness, John had a great deal of zeal, and, before that zeal was chastened by the influence and example of his Master, might have often displayed it without knowledge. At any rate, he shared with his brother in the appellation of Boanerges, or Sons of Thunder, which Mark, in his catalogue of the twelve, informs us was the surname bestowed on them by Jesus, and which seems to have reference to the heat of their temper; though by some interpreters it is supposed to signify their powers of eloquence.

In the book of Acts, we hear of James but once, after his name is given in the enumeration of the eleven apostles; and then it is to hear of his death. 'Herod the king stretched forth his hand to vex certain of the church; and he killed James, the brother of John, with the sword.' Though not the first christian martyr, he was the first of the apostles who suffered martyrdom; the first among the twelve, who, in fulfilment of that solemn prediction, was called to drink of the cup and be baptized with the baptism of their Master; the first who manifested to the world that it was beyond the power of death itself to shake their fidelity to him. If he was not spared to labor much for the church, he was soon permitted to edify it by his sufferings, and was called kindly and early to his reward in heaven.

JOHN.

We now come to John, the brother of James the Elder, and the last named, though certainly not the last in merit, of those four friends and partners, the fishermen of Bethsaida. The particulars of his call to be an apostle of Christ, have already been related, together with some other circumstances respecting him, in the lives of Peter and James. We have seen that he ardently loved his Master; that he was distinguished by that Master's peculiar regard; and that, although he was sometimes betrayed into unworthy expressions of ambition and anger, for which he was justly reprimanded, his disposition was remarkably amiable, gentle, and affectionate.

There is not much told of him, individually, till towards the closing scenes of our Saviour's ministry and life. At the last supper, which he and Peter had been sent to prepare, we are told that 'there was leaning on Jesus' bosom one of his disciples whom Jesus loved.' This disciple was John himself; who was so fond of the distinction which his Master's attachment conferred on him, or, to speak more properly, was so gratefully sensible of the value of the attachment itself, that he continually speaks of himself, in his history, as the disciple whom Jesus loved; a title which he surely would not have assumed, unless it had been really conferred on him. His place at the supper is an evidence that he was high in the favor of Jesus. He was leaning or lying on his bosom; that is, he was the next below him, and as it was the custom of the ancients to recline at their meals, his head was brought in contact with his Master's breast; a situation which used always to be reserved by the host at an entertainment, for the person whom he most honored or esteemed. It was while he was thus leaning, that Simon Peter beckoned to him that he should ask of Jesus who it was who should betray him. John did as he was requested, and Jesus showed him who the traitor was by giving Judas a sop. All this seems to have been done in private, and apart from the knowledge of the other disciples, and proves the great measure of condescension and confidence which was exercised by the Master toward this his favorite follower.

After Jesus was betrayed and seized, John is supposed to have been that other disciple, who went with Peter to the palace of the high priest, and gained him admittance there by means of his acquaintance with that dignitary. However this may be, he was the only one of the twelve who had the fortitude to attend his beloved Master to the cross. How touchingly is it manifested on this awful occasion, that the softest natures are often the noblest and most fearless too;

and that those which are apparently the most daring and masculine, may yet shrink away in the time of peril and distress. Who, in that hour of darkness—darkness in the heavens and in the hearts of men; who, in that hour of abandonment, when even the Son of God cried out that he was forsaken; who, of all his followers, were with him then, to support him by their sympathy, and prove to him their love? In the midst of scoffing soldiers, and brutal executioners, under the lowering sky, and just below the frightful cross, we behold four weeping females, and one disciple, the youngest and the gentlest of the twelve, braving the horrors of this place of blood, braving the anger of those in authority and the insults of those who do their bidding, determined to be near their friend and Master in his agonies, and ready, on the spot and at the moment, to share them. And what is it that braces up the nerves of this feeble company to such a singular pitch of fortitude and daring? The simple, but unconquerable strength of affection; the generous omnipotence of their attachment and gratitude. In the might of their love they ascend the hill of Calvary, and take their station beneath the cross; hearing nothing amidst all that tumult, but the promptings of their devoted hearts; seeing nothing but their dying Lord; remembering nothing but that he was dear to them, and that he was in misery. Oh! how loftily does courage like this, rise above that ruder and earthly courage which rushes to the battle field, and is crowned with the applauses of the world! It calls for none of those excitements and stimulants from without which goad rough spirits into madness, but relies on those resources that are within, those precious stores and holy powers which are the strength of a single and faithful breast. That is the courage of the animal; this is of the soul. It is pure; it is divine. To say all in one word, it was such as moved the complacent regard of the Saviour himself, even in the height of his sufferings. Hanging on the cross, bleeding and exhausted, yet when he saw his mother, and the disciple standing by, whom he loved, he was touched by their constancy; his thoughts were recalled to earth; the domestic affections rushed into his bosom; and with a tender care which provided at once a protection for his parent and a reward for his friend, 'he saith unto his mother, Woman, behold thy son! Then saith he to the disciple, Behold thy mother!' Where was there ever so affecting a bequest as that which was then made, when love and filial piety triumphed over suffering? Where was there ever so affecting an adoption as that which then took place, when attachment and fidelity triumphed over fear? The last earthly care of Jesus was accomplished. His mother was confided to the disciple whom he best loved. The favorite disciple eagerly accepted the honorable and precious charge; for, 'from that hour,' as we are told by himself, he 'took her unto his own home.'

The whole scene is one of unrivalled pathos. Had it taken place in a quiet chamber, and by the side of a peaceful death bed, it would have moved us; but how singularly and solemnly does it come in, a sweet and melting interlude, in the midst of that wild and appalling conflict, under the open and frowning heaven, of passion, violence, outcry, shame and agony! It is like one of those hushed pauses between the fits of a midnight storm, when the elements wait, and pity seems pleading with wrath, ere the war and the turmoil begin again.

It would appear that the enemies of our Lord were satisfied, for that time, with his destruction; for we do not read that John, or the females who were with him, suffered any harm on account of their fearless exposure. It is probable also that the prodigies which succeeded the death of Jesus, deterred his executioners from pursuing any further their work of blood.

On the morning of the resurrection, Mary Magdalene having gone to the sepulchre early, and observed that the stone was taken away from its mouth, announced this fact to Simon Peter and to John, who both ran toward the spot. John outran Peter, and came first to the sepulchre, and stooping down, saw the linen clothes in which his Master had been buried; but he went not in. Then Peter came up, and went in, and then John followed him. Why the latter did not go in immediately, does not appear from the history; nor is it easy to form a conjecture; for he was certainly equal to Peter, both in courage and attachment to his Master. Perhaps in the mere agitation of his feelings, he delayed till Peter arrived; who no sooner came up, than, with his characteristic promptness, he descended into the sepulchre where his crucified Lord had been deposited, in order, it may be, that he might ask forgiveness even of his remains, for having so shamefully denied him.

A passage in John's own account of this visit to the tomb of Jesus, renders it probable that he was the first person who believed in the resurrection of his Lord. 'Then went in also that other disciple, who came first to the sepulchre, and he saw, and believed;' that is, believed that Jesus had arisen from the dead. Nor is this obvious interpretation contradicted by the succeeding verse; 'For as yet they knew not the scripture, that he must rise again from the dead.' By the word 'they' is not meant Peter and John particularly, but all the disciples. The belief was not yet received among them, that their Master was to rise from the dead; and therefore it was a remarkable circumstance, and one worthy of being recorded, that John was the first who remembered the predictions of Jesus, and acknowledged their fulfilment. So unprepared were the disciples for his resurrection, that Peter, who first saw that the tomb was empty, did not think of ascribing the fact to its true cause. It was into the mind of the beloved disciple that the light first broke. He first believed the glorious truth, that death was vanquished by the Son of God, and that Jesus of Nazereth was the Prince of Life.

When Jesus appeared to his disciples for the third time after his resurrection, and at the close of his solemn address to Peter, intimated to him that he should die a violent death, that disciple, seeing John just behind, desired to know what his lot was to be. The answer of Jesus was, 'If I will that he tarry till I come, what is that to thee?' This answer caused a saying to go abroad that John should not die; but we shall presently see what was the probable meaning of our Saviour's prophetic words.

In the book of Acts, we again meet with John in company with Peter, when the lame man was healed at the Beautiful Gate. This act of mercy and divine power occasioned their imprisonment. They were brought together before the council of priests and scribes; they were both charged to teach no more in the name of Jesus; they both nobly refused to obey; and they were both dismissed by the council, who were afraid at that time to punish them. It is pleasing to see those who had formerly been partners in a lowly, but honest calling, thus continuing to toil hand in hand, in their more exalted profession of fishers of men. It is an exhibition of christian friendship, which should not pass unnoticed. On one other occasion they were united in their holy labors; when they were sent by the apostles on the mission to Samaria; after which we hear no more of John in the historical portion of the scriptures.

All early testimonies agree, however, that he was spared to a great age, and outlived all the apostles; earnestly occupied, while his strength remained, in the service of his Master and the promotion of his religion. It is said by some writers, that he preached to the Parthians; and it is certain that he dwelt for some time at Ephesus, where Mary, his adopted mother, whom he had constantly taken care of, according to the solemn testament of her own son, is supposed to have ended her days.

In the year of our Lord, 70, and when John was

about seventy years of age, the destruction of Jerusalem, by Titus, took place. It is understood by commentators generally, that it was this event to which Jesus referred, when he intimated that John should tarry till his coming. If so, the prediction was remarkably fulfilled; for this disciple was the only one of the twelve who lived to see that once proud city utterly overthrown, her glorious temple destroyed, and the very ground on which it stood, ploughed up by the hands of the heathen.

Between the years 90 and 100, and in the reign of the emperor Domitian, he was banished to the Isle of Patmos, in the Egean sea. Here he wrote the book of the Revelation; and here he remained, till the death of Domitian, whose successor, Nerva, recalled those who had been banished for their faith in the preceding reign. He then returned to Ephesus, where he is said to have written his Gospel, and where he died a natural and peaceful death, at the extreme old age of one hundred years. According to Epiphanius, he died at the age of ninetyfour, in the one hundredth year of the christian era; a calculation which makes him six years younger than our Lord. But others say that he lived to the age which was first mentioned; and others again assert that his life was protracted beyond that term. All agree, however, that he was more than ninety at his death.

He left several writings behind him, which have been preserved in the church from age to age, and which of themselves bear witness to the affectionate mildness of his character. His Gospel was written after the three others; which accounts for its omitting many things which they relate, and relating many things which they omit. It is John alone who tells us of the resurrection of Lazarus; of Christ's washing his disciples' feet; and especially of those divine discourses which he held with them just before he was betrayed, and which were treasured up in the faithful memory and kindred heart of the beloved disciple, with a minuteness which proves how deeply he had been impressed by them.

The book of the Revelation, which antiquity also ascribes to John, though not with an entirely unanimous voice, has both exercised and baffled as much critical ingenuity and research as ever were bestowed on any writing in the world. The majority of its interpreters have regarded it as a series of particular prophecies; and these supposed prophecies have been applied to so many events, past and to come, that the reader is at last convinced that the truth does not even lie between the differing hypothesis. It may be, that its splendid visions are really of a prophetic nature, and that they are not yet accomplished. But perhaps the most rational theory is that which several learned men have adopted, and which supposes that the whole book of the Revelation is only a general prediction of the glorious success of Christianity in the world, and its triumph over its numerous foes, without any reference to the political condition of certain states and empires, or to the downfall of particular hierarchies or heresies. This opinion has been explained and supported by the German professor, Eichorn, in a commentary on Revelation; and in earlier times had been maintained by able expositors, and espoused by no less a man than the poet Milton. But whatever difference there may be concerning the intention of this book, there can be none with regard to its composition. It is undoubtedly a magnificent specimen of holy poetry; and reminds us more constantly and strongly of the sublimest of the Jewish prophecies, than any other book in the canon of the New Testament.

Beside the two works already named, we have three epistles appearing in the christian scriptures as the productions of the apostle John. That he wrote the one which is called the first, there has never been any dispute; it is universally, and by the best authorities, ascribed to him. But the genuineness of the two others was questioned at a very early period; though the balance in their favor appeared so great, that they were admitted into our present collection of sacred books. The controversy need not trouble us, however; as the two latter epistles, beside being very short, contain nothing of consequence which is not likewise contained in substance, and almost precisely in expression, in the first. This first epistle exhibits in a more striking light than do the rest of his writings, his great amiableness of disposition. It is throughout an exhortation; an exhortation from the heart and soul and mind and strength of the writer, to pure, exalted, christian benevolence; and its whole drift and spirit may be expressed in this single passage from the fourth chapter; 'God is love; and he that dwelleth in love dwelleth in God, and God in him.'

To John, as well as to most of the apostles of Christ, are attributed by antiquity both writings and actions which are probably apocryphal and fabulous. It would be useless for me even to give the titles of the former. Of the traditions of his actions and miracles, one of the most generally known and quoted, is the story, that, during the persecution under Domitian, and just before the exile of John to Patmos, he was brought to Rome, and there thrown into a cauldron of boiling oil, from which he came out altogether unhurt. In the pictures of him by the old painters, he is often represented as holding a cup or goblet, from which a serpent is rearing its head. This accompaniment refers to another legend respecting him, by one Prochorus, who tells us that some heretics having presented the apostle with a cup of poisoned liquor, he made the sign of the cross over it, and all the venom was immediately expelled from the vessel, embodied in the visible form of a serpent.

Stories of this kind would naturally be multiplied in that, or indeed in any age, concerning persons whose lives were singularly out of the common course, and who were in reality gifted with the power of working miracles. The ancient writers and fathers were too apt to promulgate such legends, without distinguishing them, as carefully as they ought to have done, from accounts which were worthy of credit; and the church, finding how ready, and even eager, the multitude were to receive every tale of wonder, made it a part of its policy to cherish their credulity and strengthen their delusion. But we, who are of a more simple taste, require no such means to interest us in the history of a person, in every way so interesting as the 'disciple whom Jesus loved.'

PHILIP.

The fifth named on Matthew's catalogue of the apostles, is Philip. He was a native of Bethsaida, and consequently a townsman of the four partners, whose histories I have already told. We have no certain intelligence of his parentage or condition, though he was probably in the same rank of life with Peter and Andrew, James and John, and perhaps of the same profession. The day after Peter and Andrew had become disciples of Christ, we read that 'Jesus would go forth into Galilee, and findeth Philip, and saith unto him, Follow me.' And we then read, further, that 'Philip findeth Nathaniel, and saith unto him, We have found him of whom Moses in the law, and the prophets, did write, Jesus of Nazareth, the son of Joseph.' His conduct in this instance is like that of Andrew; as he manifested the same readiness to acknowledge Jesus as the Messiah, and the same zeal to make known his discovery to others.

This faith and zeal, however, do not continue to be, if we may judge from what little the Gospels relate of

Philip, so firm and ardent afterwards as they seem to have been at first. When Jesus, in order to prove him, asked him where bread enough could be bought to feed the five thousand who were gathered together on the mountain, Philip, either not remembering the miraculous power of his Master, or not yet fully convinced of its reality, entered into a calculation, and returned, for answer, that two hundred pennyworth of bread would not be sufficient to supply every one with a little. And at the last supper, when our Lord was discoursing so divinely to his disciples, and had said to them that if they had known him properly, they would have known his Father, whom very soon they would both know and see, Philip was so entirely unconscious of his meaning, and so blind, notwithstanding his long intimacy with Jesus, so blind to the presence and agency of God in this, his beloved Son, as to say to his Master, 'Lord, show us the Father, and it sufficeth us.' Grieved at his dullness and insensibility, Jesus returns that sadly reproachful answer, 'Have I been so long time with you, and yet hast thou not known me, Philip? He that hath seen me, hath seen the Father; and how sayest thou then, Show us the Father? Believest thou not that I am in the Father, and the Father in me? The words that I speak unto you, I speak not of myself; but the Father that dwelleth in me, he doeth the works.' As if he had said, Is it not evident to you that the power which you have seen me exert, is more than human power? that the wisdom which you have so long been hearing from my lips, is more than human wisdom? that the

Father must have been with me, and in me, all this time, or I could not have thus acted and spoken? How can you then, who have been one of my constant companions, how can you say, Show us the Father? As a Jew, you certainly do not expect to see God in person; and how can you behold a brighter manifestation of his image and attributes than that which you have so long beheld in me? You do not know me, Philip, neither me nor my Father.

This instance of the apostle's incredulity and slowness of apprehension, does not prove that he was more incredulous and dull than his brethren; it only shows how small the impression was which the extraordinary intructions and actions of Jesus had as yet produced on the whole twelve. They entered into his service with the Jewish ideas of a Messiah; and now, when he was just about to leave them, they were almost as ignorant of the spirituality of his kingdom, as when they first joined themselves to him.

Nothing further is said in the sacred histories to assist us in elucidating Philip's character. The book of Acts relates nothing concerning him; for we must not confound Philip the Apostle, with Philip the Deacon, or Philip the Evangelist, both of whom are there mentioned. Eusebius informs us that he was a married man; that he had several daughters; that he preached in Phrygia, and that he was buried at Hieropolis.

BARTHOLOMEW.

The next in order of the twelve, is Bartholomew. Respecting him there is a still greater dearth of information, than there is respecting Philip; for there is absolutely nothing told of him in the New Testament, unless we resort to the supposition, which many scholars have adopted, that he is the same person with Nathaniel. In favor of this supposition there are several arguments, which form together a body of strong presumptive evidence.

It is observed, in the first place, that the evangelists Matthew, Mark, and Luke, who all place Bartholomew on their catalogues of the apostles, never mention Nathaniel; and that John, who gives the particulars of Nathaniel's conversation with our Lord, never mentions Bartholomew. Secondly, it is remarked, that Nathaniel is introduced, in the company of several apostles, in the twentyfirst chapter of John's Gospel, in such a manner as to lead us to suppose that he likewise might be one. The passage is that which relates the appearance of Jesus, after his resurrection, at the sea of Tiberias; on which occasion Peter swam to him from the vessel in which he and the rest were fishing. The disciples, who were present, are thus named; 'There were together, Simon Peter, and Thomas, called Didymus, and Nathaniel of Cana in Galilee, and the sons of Zebedee, and two other of his disciples.' Thirdly, the difference in the two names, which may at first appear to be an argument against this supposition, is rather in its favor. Bartholomew signifies the son of Tolmai, just as Bartimeus, the blind man whom Jesus restored to sight, signifies the son of Timeus; *bar* being the Hebrew word for son. Nathaniel, therefore, might have also been called Bartholomew, after his father, just as Simon was also called Barjonas, after his father. Bartholomew could hardly have been the only name of the apostle, because it is a patromymic; and when circumstances agree so well, why might not his first name have been Nathaniel? That John never calls Nathanniel by the other name of Bartholomew, is no proof that he had no other name; for Matthew, though his other name was Levi, never calls himself by that name, throughout the whole of his own Gospel. And finally, we are led naturally to the presumption that Nathaniel must have been an apostle, not only by the circumstance of his being named in the midst of four apostles, but by the tenor of the conversation which Jesus held with him, and the probability that he was one of the very earliest disciples.

If we are convinced by these considerations that Bartholomew was the same person with Nathaniel, we of course know something of his character and history. We view him as an inhabitant of Cana, in Galilee; as called to be an apostle on the same day with Philip, by whom he was introduced to Jesus; and as one who was characterized by the Saviour, and therefore deservedly, as an 'Israelite indeed, in whom there was no guile.'

According to some ancient accounts, Bartholomew preached the Gospel in the Indies, in Arabia, and Persia, and died in Albana, a city on the Caspian Sea. There is an uncertain tradition that he was flayed alive.

THOMAS.

The seventh of the twelve is Thomas. In the Gospel of John, he is styled 'Thomas called Didymus,' but every where else, simply Thomas. It is probable that Didymus is merely an interpretation into Greek of the Hebrew word Thomas, as they both mean *a twin*. And it may be that he really was what his name designates him to have been. But we have no certain accounts whatever of his early life, nor of the early period of his apostleship.

The first mention which is made of him, is on a most interesting occasion, and when he appears in a most interesting light. Shortly after our Lord had escaped from the hands of the Jews, who were about to stone him, and had gone away beyond Jordan, the sisters of Lazarus, his friend, sent to him, informing him that their brother was sick. Jesus remained two days, after hearing this intelligence, in the place where he was; for it was his intention, not to rescue, but to restore Lazarus from death, that God might be the more glorified; and then he said to his disciples, 'Let us go into Judea again.' His disciples earnestly sought to dissuade him from this, as they thought it, rash determination, and said unto him, 'Master, the Jews of late sought to stone thee; and goest thou thither again?' In answer to this expostulation, Jesus tells them, in figurative speech, that what he had to do must be done in its due season, and before the appropriated time was past; and then he adds, 'Our friend Lazarus sleepeth; but I go that I may awake him out of sleep.' The disciples, understanding him literally, answer, that if Lazarus was sleeping, he would recover, and therefore it was unnecessary to incur danger, merely for the sake of seeing him. 'Then said Jesus unto them, plainly, Lazarus is dead. And I am glad for your sakes that I was not there, to the intent ye may believe; nevertheless, let us go unto him.' It is at this crisis, when the apostles seem to be hesitating between the sense of imminent danger, and the feeling of duty to their Master, the one holding them back, and the other urging them forward, that Thomas advances, faithful, bold, and with a mind made up to abide by Jesus at all hazards, and says unto his fellow disciples, 'Let us also go, that we may die with him.' His intrepidity in this case had its effect, no doubt, on his brethren; for they all went to Bethany, the village of Lazarus, which was only about two miles from Jerusalem, and the result was one of the most remarkable and important miracles of our Lord; which was soon followed indeed, as the disciples had feared, and as he had foreseen, by his own violent death.

Thomas is again introduced as one of the speakers

on the night of the last supper. As Jesus was discoursing to his disciples, endeavouring to prepare them for his approaching departure, and to lead them to the sublime and consoling truths of immortality, he said to them, 'Whither I go ye know, and the way you know.' Thomas, who, no more than the rest, could believe, that the Messiah was to die, and to be taken from the world, before he had achieved his expected glories, and the deliverance of Israel, said to him, 'Lord, we know not whither thou goest; and how can we know the way?' His thoughts had not accompanied his Master's thoughts; they were yet on the earth, groping about there after a destination and a path, though Jesus was pointing so plainly to the mansions of another world, and the true and spiritual way which led to them. And it was immediately afterwards that Philip, too, uttered those words of ignorance, which we have just now considered, and which show how much that light was needed, which was soon to break in upon them all.

Once more we hear of Thomas, in a manner which marks his character with some strong lines, and particularly distinguishes his life. On the evening of the resurrection, our Saviour came and stood in the midst of the disciples, and showed them the wounds in his hands and side, and satisfied them that he was indeed risen from the dead. But Thomas was not then with them, and when they told him that they had seen the Lord, he replied, that unless he not only should see those wounds, but be allowed also to touch them and put his hand in them, he would not believe. There is a boldness and even obstinacy in this resolution, which at first is apt to offend us; but on reflection we may find that it was neither harsh nor unreasonable. He could not have refused his belief as he did, through a want of respect or affection for his Master; because he had but a short time before expressed his readiness to die with him. Neither did he hold in too slight regard the testimony of his brethren, considering the circumstances; for it was no common matter to which they testified; in almost any other case he would have believed their report, or the report of a single one of their number, but now, the event which they related was too marvellous in itself, and too momentous in its consequences, to be received on the witness of men who might not wish to deceive, but who nevertheless might themselves be deceived or mistaken; and he would trust to nothing but his own senses to bring him decisive evidence of an occurrence on which the direction of his whole future life depended.

He thought too, no doubt, that he ought to be satisfied of this wonderful fact as well as the rest of the disciples, and in the same way; and he was unquestionably right in so thinking. If he was hereafter to journey through the world, teaching and asserting, with all his powers, and in the face of every peril, the resurrection of Jesus the Christ, it was needful that he should possess a deep conviction of the reality of that event, such a conviction as, in the capacity of a companion, friend, pupil, and apostle of Jesus, he ought to have, and such a conviction as the world would surely require of him. The miracle had just occurred, as his brethren told him; if so, why should not he, standing in the same situation as they did, and to whom its truth was as important as to them, why should not he have the same evidence as they did; nay, why should he not have more? Why should he not, not only on his own account, but as their representative, demand the opportunity of clearing away every shadow of doubt which might rest on so splendid a truth, both by seeing his risen Lord as they had, and touching him with his hands as they had not?

If we regard the incredulity of Thomas in this light, we shall see nothing improper in it, and shall be disposed to grant, that it was no greater than, in his situation, was natural and justifiable. In this conclusion we are countenanced by the conduct of our Saviour himself, who neither refuses to show himself to his doubting disciple, nor manifests any displeasure at his freedom or his unbelief; for the narration of the occurrence is thus continued by St John: 'And after eight days, again his disciples were within, and Thomas with them. Then came Jesus, the doors being shut, and stood in the midst, and said, Peace be unto you. Then saith he to Thomas, Reach hither thy finger, and behold my hands; and reach hither thy hand, and thrust it into my side; and be not faithless but believing.' Startled, doubtless, by the sudden appearance of his Master, and affected too by the kind and assuring manner in which he is bid to satisfy his doubts completely, Thomas broke out into the exclamation of wonder and acknowledgment, 'My Lord and my

God!' His doubts were entirely overcome, his faith was now as ardent and lively as before his distrust had been cold; and his testimony to the reality of the resurrection is perhaps more valuable than any other single testimony, because it was rendered under such peculiar circumstances, and by one so honest and so sturdy in avowing his scruples, and so candid in resigning them.

The exclamation of Thomas, quoted above, has held so conspicuous a place, and been so often brought forward in theological controversy, that I must necessarily dwell for a moment on the consideration of its import. By many, though by no means by all of those who hold the doctrine of the perfect equality of the Son with the Father, it has been adduced as a scripture proof of that equality; as an acknowledgment by the apostle of the godhead and supreme divinity of Jesus Christ. To this interpretation of the passage, there seem to me to be insurmountable objections. In the first place, the question of the deity of Christ has no concern with the event. It was not to be satisfied of the deity, but of the resurrection of his Master, that Thomas required his appearance; and it was to convince him of that resurrection, that his Master condescended to appear to him. 'Except I shall see in his hands the print of the nails, and put my finger into the print of the nails, and thrust my hand into his side, I will not believe.' Believe what? What the disciples had just told him, certainly, that they had seen the Lord, that he was truly alive, not that he was truly God. Secondly, it is difficult to conceive how the appearance of Jesus in a human form, just as he had always appeared before, and with bodily wounds, just as he had been taken from the cross, that is, as a man in all respects, could have convinced his disciple, and that disciple a Jew, that he was the eternal God. The miracle of the resurrection itself could not have had this effect, because Thomas had often witnessed the miracles of his Master, without once confessing that he was God; and no other evidence was at this time offered. Thirdly, if Jesus was on this occasion acknowledged to be God, it might be expected that the writer of the narrative should take some notice of the circumstance; but what are his words, immediately after relating this event? 'These are written, that ye might believe that Jesus is *the Christ, the Son of God;*' not God himself. Fourthly, the exclamation itself is abrupt, and without any connexion to determine precisely its meaning. It might not have been addressed to Jesus at all, but to God alone; or the first appellation might have been addressed to him, and the second to Heaven; it was an exclamation, in short, of wonder, of extatic wonder, of extatic gratitude, and just such a one as any of us would be likely to utter on witnessing a similar marvel; such, for instance as the resurrection of a dear friend from the grave. Fifthly, if the whole exclamation was really addressed to Jesus, the term God might well have been applied, according to known Jewish usage, and in its lower sense, to one who now had manifested undeniably that he was the Messiah, the Prince of Peace, the Son of God, and the King of Israel. Lastly, the answer of Jesus himself excludes the supposition that he was addressed as the Supreme God. For he said unto his disciple, 'Thomas, because thou hast seen me, thou hast believed; blessed are they that have not seen, and yet have believed.' Now this must mean, 'Because thou hast seen me here alive, after my crucifixion and burial, thou hast believed that I am raised from the dead; and it is well; but blessed are they who cannot have such evidence of the senses, and yet shall believe in the glorious truth, from your evidence, and that of your brethren.' He could not have meant, that they were blessed, who, though they had not seen him, yet had believed that he was God; because there is no connexion between the propositions; because the fact of the resurrection of Jesus cannot, to the mind of any one, be of itself a proof of his Deity; and, because no one thinks of requiring to see God, in order to believe that he exists. In conclusion, it must be remembered, that these considerations are so obvious, that they have been fully adopted by some of those who still have professed their belief, founded on other evidence, of the Deity of Christ.

It cannot be doubted that the decided and resolute character of Thomas, fitted him eminently for his apostolic duties. But the accounts which we have of his life and works after the ascension of his Master, though sufficiently copious, are worthy of but little faith. It would seem, however, that he travelled through many parts of the Indies; that he suffered martyrdom, and that his body was carried to Edessa, and there interred.

MATTHEW.

Matthew places himself the eighth on his list, and styles himself 'the Publican.' This avowal of his profession is at once a proof of his humility and his good sense. He had the meekness to set himself down exactly what he was, notwithstanding the contempt which the confession might bring upon him; and he had the wisdom to perceive that there was no rank or occupation in life, however low, which could change the nature of true worth, or really disgrace an honest and virtuous man.

To the Jews, above all other people, *publican* was an odious name. There is a use of this word among us, a low and improper use, which has nothing to do with its true signification and its scripture sense; for a publican does not mean, in the Gospels, an innkeeper, but a taxgatherer, or a receiver of the tribute imposed by government. The Romans employed these receivers of tribute or publicans, in all their provinces, and among the rest, in Judea. Now, to pay tribute was not only a constant acknowledgment and badge of subjection and servitude, but to the Jews it was something more galling still, because it wounded their religious as well as their political pride. It was a thought of pure, unmitigated bitterness, that the people of God should thus pass periodically under the hated yoke of idolaters, and, as they would call them in their haughty exclusiveness, barbarians. The office itself being thus detestable, it may be conceived how those persons must have been looked upon who held and exercised it.

There were two orders, however, among the publicans; the receivers general, who had deputies under them, and these deputies themselves. The former were usually selected from the best classes of society; but the latter were reckoned ignoble and contemptible, even by the Gentiles, and were, as a body, vulgar, rapacious, and unmerciful. Some one asked Theocritus, which was the most cruel of all beasts? and he answered, 'Among the beasts of the wilderness, the bear and the lion; among the beasts of the city, the publican and the parasite.' Of the higher order of publicans at Jerusalem, one is probably mentioned in the Gospel of Luke, by the name of Zacchæus, who is there said to be 'the chief among the publicans,' and a rich man. Of the lower order, were those who are so frequently classed in the scriptures with sinners; and of this order was Matthew. They were all, high and low, for the reasons just given, regarded with abhorrence by the Jews, and treated as a profane and outcast set of people. 'Let him be unto thee *as a heathen man and a publican,*' is a phrase which expresses strongly the universal ban which was suspended over them. We are told that though a publican might be a Jew, he was hardly recognised as such by his countrymen; that he was not allowed to enter the temple; nor give testimony in courts of justice; that the gifts, even, which his devotion might prompt him to offer, were rejected from the altar of Jehovah, as unclean and abominable.

Bearing these things in mind, we can now estimate the selfdenial of the apostle, who, with a firm pen, could write himself down, 'Matthew, *the Publican.*'

In the second chapter of Mark, he is said to be the son of Alpheus; but whether this Alpheus is the same with the father of James the Less, or another individual, is uncertain. His place of residence was in Capernaum, or somewhere near it, on the sea of Tiberias. Though he constantly calls himself Matthew, he is called Levi by the other evangelists; and it is for this reason that Levi and Matthew have been supposed by some celebrated scholars to be two different persons. But the circumstances of Matthew's call to be a disciple, as related in his own Gospel, are so precisely similar to those which attend the call of Levi, as related in the Gospels of Mark and Luke, that the predominant opinion has always been, that Matthew and Levi were only two names for one and the same person.

Though a publican, of an inferior rank, belonging to a class of men who were considered vile, and who generally deserved their reputation, Matthew was an upright and religious man; and there was *one* of his countrymen, if there were no more, who could separate the man from the profession, and fearlessly engage him for his companion and friend. It was he who saw him sitting in his place of business, or at the receipt of custom, as it is called, and said unto him, 'Follow me.' These were words, which, from those lips, could not be uttered in vain; and the humble publican, who probably had before heard the discourses of Jesus, and heard them with admiration, and seen also some of the wonders which he had done, immediately arose and followed him.

Our Saviour, after having called Matthew, went to his house; and there his new disciple prepared a supper for him; and many publicans and sinners, the former associates of Matthew, came and sat down with Jesus and his disciples. When some Pharisees, who were present, saw this, they said to the disciples, 'Why eateth your Master with publicans and sinners? But when Jesus heard that, he said unto them, They who are whole need not a physician, but they who are sick. But go ye, and learn what that meaneth, I will have mercy, and not sacrifice; for I am not come to call the righteous, but sinners to repentance.'

In both of these incidents, the spirit of Christianity and the character of its founder are conspicuous. The call of a publican to be a follower of Christ and a herald of his religion, was a sign of the sublime superiority of the new faith, in its impartiality and mercy, over the bigotries of the old; and evinces the discernment and the independence of Jesus, in selecting a worthy disciple from an order of men, among whom common opinion had pronounced that there was no worth to be found. And in sitting down to eat, that greatest token of familiarity, in the house of this publican, and with a mixed company of reputed sinners, Jesus again manifests the universal benevolence of his temper and his doctrine. To the hypocritical Pharisees, it was indeed a strange and scandalous thing, that one who set up as the Messiah of Israel, and the purifier of its ordinances, should take a publican to be a pupil, and break bread with other publicans and notorious sinners; but how well are their narrow prejudices and their supercilious and uncharitable self righteousness rebuked by the stedfast reply of the Saviour! 'The religion which I would inculcate,' as the reply may be paraphrased, 'embraces in its pure mercy the whole family of man; it draws no impassable line between the privileged and the profane; it leaves none to despair of heaven's favor and acceptance;—if ye are perfect, if ye are whole, my errand is not to you; go; go to your temple, and perform your rites; but when there, study the meaning of that scripture, I will have mercy and not sacrifice. As for these, they are sick; they need a physician, and I must heal them; ye yourselves say that they are sinners, and why shall I not call them to repentance, and save them?'

With what has been now told from the Gospels concerning Matthew, we must rest contented; but even from these slight memorials we shall gain a highly favorable impression of his character. In his depressed condition as a publican, he seems to have learned the valuable lesson of humility; and thus to have become 'almost a Christian,' before he was a follower of Christ. Among his vile companions, whom public obloquy had made yet more vile than their habits and their occupation would have made them, he was upright, honest, merciful, uncontaminated. His integrity appears doubly bright by contrast, amidst the dark examples and fearful temptations which were all around it like clouds; and his virtue, reared among quicksands and waves, proved, simply by its being and standing there, how very deeply and strongly its foundations were laid. It is further to be remarked, that though he was the writer of one of the Gospel histories, he says nothing more of himself than that he was called to follow Jesus while he was sitting in his office, and that he afterwards entertained his Master at his house; and this latter circumstance he only mentions in order that he may introduce the answer of Jesus to the Pharisees. We could have no better evidence than this, of his disinterestedness and modesty.

His Gospel is every where distinguished by plain good sense and manly simplicity. It was written, as some of the ancients say, fifteen years after the ascension of our Saviour, or as others affirm, yet seven years earlier. Although some critics have advanced the opinion that Luke's Gospel was the first which was written, the general voice of antiquity is against them, and a majority also, I believe, of the moderns. So that the Gospel of Matthew really stands, in all probability, where a place is given to it in our Bibles, the first in order of the four evangelical histories.

Another circumstance respecting it, which the earliest ecclesiastical authors record, and which, though it has been controverted, is most probably a fact, is, that we do not possess it in the language in which it was originally composed. It was written by Matthew, according to the best testimony, at Jerusalem, on purpose for the Jewish converts, and in that modern dialect or species of Hebrew which was the common language, at that time, of Palestine. The Gospel in that language has been lost, it is supposed, irretrievably. That which we have, is a translation of it into Greek, made very soon after the original was composed. There is no reason to challenge its exact faithfulness to the original; and some have even supposed that Matthew himself was the author of this Greek rendering of his own Hebrew Gospel. The predominant opinion is, however, that the name of the translator, and the Gospel which he translated, are alike unknown and undiscoverable. Though we may be allowed to regret that we cannot look on the very words which this excellent apostle used in narrating, for our exceeding benefit, the life and actions of his Master, yet our faith ought not to be in the least disturbed by the loss, while there remains to us a translation of his history, so manifestly ancient, complete, and true.

Matthew is said to have carried the religion of Jesus into Parthia and Ethiopia, and to have suffered martyrdom at Naddaber, in the latter country. We are told also that his remains were brought to Bithynia, and from thence to Salernum, in the kingdom of

Naples, where they were discovered in the year 1080, and where a church was built for them by duke Robert, in the pontificate of Gregory VII. We can readily believe that relics were thus found and honored, which were declared, and by many supposed, to be the body of the apostle; but that they really were so, we are at perfect liberty to question and to deny.

JAMES THE LESS.

Next to his own name, Matthew writes that of 'James, the son of Alpheus;' who is also called, in the Gospel of Mark, 'James the less,' or the younger, to distinguish him from the other apostle of the same name, James the brother of John, who was older than he; or it may be that he was of small stature, and therefore named 'the less.' His mother's name was Mary. She was one of the Marys who were present at the crucifixion of our Saviour; and appears to have been the sister of Mary the mother of Jesus. In the Gospel of Mark she is called 'Mary, the mother of James the Less and of Joses.' In a parallel passage of John's Gospel, she is mentioned as follows. 'There stood by the cross of Jesus, his mother, *and his mother's sister, Mary the wife of Cleophas*, and Mary Magdalene.' From these passages the inference is justly drawn, that James the Less was the first cousin of Jesus. He is expressly called the son of Alpheus and of Mary, and as Mary who was the wife of Alpheus, which is only the Greek pronunciation of the Hebrew name Cleophas, is also termed in the same passage the sister of our Lord's mother, he is consequently our Lord's cousin. He is the same person who is mentioned by Paul, when he says, in his Epistle to the Galatians, 'But other of the apostles saw I none, save James the Lord's brother.' To account for this appellation, it must be observed that the Jews were accustomed to include all near relations under the general name of brethren. And we may also remark, that though it appears strange that Mary should be the sister of Mary, it was not uncommon among the Jews, that two sisters of the same family should bear the same name. James is likewise enumerated among the Lord's brethren by the Jews, when they asked in astonishment, 'Is not this the carpenter's son? is not his mother called Mary? and his brethren, James, and Joses, and Simon, and Judas?' Of these four sons, three were apostles of Jesus; and the other one, Joses, or Joseph, was probably a disciple; as was Cleophas too, or Alpheus, the father of this christian family.

No particulars are related of James in the Gospels; but honorable mention is made of him in the book of Acts, and the Epistles of Paul. Perhaps his youth and his modesty, together with his near relationship to Jesus, operated upon him to be silent and inactive during the life of the Saviour, though afterwards his talents and worth made him conspicuous. He appears to have resided constantly at Jerusalem, and to have been president or bishop of the church there. All antiquity affirms this, and scripture gives it good countenance. Thus we are told in the twelfth chapter of Acts, that when Peter had been miraculously delivered from the prison into which he had been thrown by Herod, who had just slain the other James, he went to the house of a believing family, and said to those who were there; 'Go, show these things unto James, and the brethren.' James is evidently spoken of here, as having a precedence among the brethren. Again, in the fifteenth chapter of the same book, he appears to have been the presiding member of the Council of Jerusalem, of which I have before had occasion to speak, and which decided that the Gentiles were to be received, on their conversion, into the full privileges of the christian church, without being obliged to undergo the ceremony of circumcision. It has been observed that though Peter spoke first on this occasion, James spoke last, and gave his opinion or 'sentence' with regard to the most proper course to be pursued, and that the letter or result of the council was chiefly modelled upon his words. From these circumstances it has been concluded that he was the moderator or president of this first christian council, and that this rank was probably conceded to him on account of his being the presiding apostle or bishop of Jerusalem, in which place the council was convened. Peter, as it may be remembered, agreed with James entirely in this case; but, though in some sense chief of the apostles, it is evident that when the church came to be enlarged and settled, he did not possess any general supreme authority, but, as in the present council, was regarded, and regarded himself, as in subordination to the local authorities. The speech of James is replete with good sense, dignity, and a spirit of charity and forbearance, and sufficiently indicates the wisdom of his brethren in making him bishop or overseer of the christian church of Jerusalem.

In the twentyfirst chapter of Acts there is also a particular mention of James, which corroborates the preceding proofs of his consequence in the church. In an account there given of the journey of Paul and his company to Jerusalem, with the collections for the saints in Judea, the writer says, 'And when we were come to Jerusalem, the brethren received us gladly. And the day following, Paul went in with us unto James; and all the elders were present.' James could hardly have been singled out by name in this passage, for any other reason than because he was the chief person at this convocation of the elders.

To all this evidence of the standing of James and the high consideration in which he was held, the testimony of Paul himself is to be added. One passage has already been adduced from the first chapter of his epistle to the Galatians. In the second chapter, Paul says, 'And when James, Cephas, and John, who seemed to be pillars, perceived the grace that was given unto me, they gave to me and Barnabas the right hands of fellowship, that we should go unto the heathen, and they unto the circumcision.' Here it is to be noted, that James is not only called one of the pillars of the church, but is placed at the head of the three; even before Cephas, or Peter. At the same time we ought to observe, that ecclesiastical rank was by no means, in those primitive times, that thing of name and pomp and prerogative that it has since been made in most of the churches of Christendom; for if James had been the bishop of Jerusalem in the same sense in which the title is now applied, Paul would never have said of him and the others, that they 'seemed to be pillars;' an expression which plainly signifies, that they appeared, as far as he could judge, to be the first men in the church. In truth, a bishop in those days was only a moderator among brethren and equals; appointed to the office by them, and appointed to it for his superior gifts and attainments.

Once more, and in this same chapter, is James mentioned. Paul, in relating the vacillating conduct of Peter, with regard to eating with the Gentiles, says, in the words which I have already quoted in Peter's life, 'Before that certain came from James, he did eat with the Gentiles; but when they were come, he withdrew and separated himself.' Here again is James spoken of as a person of consideration and authority.

Thus far do the scriptures inform us of the life and character of James the Less. Ancient ecclesiastical writers have much to say of his virtues and wisdom, and of the respect which they procured for him, both among the faithful and the unbelieving. The Jews, we are told, were unbounded in their admiration of him; insomuch, that, as Jerome affirms, they used to strive to touch the hem of his garment. On account of his remarkable integrity, he obtained another surname beside that which is given to him in the scriptures, and was called James the Just. Some go so far as to say, that he was allowed to enter into the Holy of Holies of the Jewish temple; but this must be a fiction. It is a fiction, however, which, together with other similar ones, shows that there must have been a foundation for them in the high character and reputation of this apostle.

The circumstances of his death are differently stated. Josephus, the Jewish historian, is supposed to relate it in the following passage from the twentieth book of his Antiquities, which I give in the translation of L'Estrange. 'The Ananus we are now speaking of, [who had recently been raised to the high priesthood by Agrippa,] was naturally fierce and hardy; by sect, a Sadducee, the most censorious and uncharitable sort of people upon the face of the earth. This being his way and opinion, he took his opportunity, in the interval betwixt the death of Festus and the arrival of his successor Albinus, who was as yet but upon the way, to call a council together, with the assistance of the judges, and to cite James, the brother of Jesus, which was called Christ, with some others, to appear before them, and answer to a charge of blasphemy, and breach of the law; whereupon they were condemned, and delivered up to be stoned.' The account proceeds to say that all the sober and conscientious part of the city were so much offended with this high handed way of acting, that they sent a representation of it, with a remonstrance, both to king Agrippa, and to Albinus; the consequence of which was, that Ananus was deposed by Agrippa from the pontificate. This passage would be decisive, were it not that several learned men question the genuineness of the words, 'the brother of Jesus which was called Christ.' Lardner thinks that they are an interpolation, and inclines to the account given by Eusebius, in the second book of his Ecclesiastical History; who says, 'When Paul had appealed to Cæsar, and had been sent to Rome by Festus, the Jews, who had aimed at his death, being disappointed in that design, turned their rage against James the Lord's brother, who had been appointed by the apostles, bishop of Jerusalem;' and then he goes on to state, that James was killed in a popular tumult. If this narrative is the true one, it makes the death of the apostle a year or two earlier than it is dated by Josephus; but at any rate we may safely fix it somewhere about the year 60, and eight or ten years before the destruction of Jerusalem. He was buried, according to Gregory, bishop of Tours, on Mount Olivet, in a tomb which he had built for himself.

There is one epistle, among the canonical books of the New Testament, which is very generally ascribed to James the Less, the brother or cousin of Jesus. It is a noble exhortation, full of good sense and spirit, dignified, independent, and explicit. Its value is of the highest estimate, both as it is an unreserved declaration of the intrinsic merit and importance of good works or virtue, and as it contains a most fearless, indignant, and forcible denunciation of the reigning vices and follies of the generation to whom the apostle wrote. A common opinion among the ancient writers of the church, is, that the first part of it was composed expressly to explain those passages of Paul's epistles which seem to slight good works, and make every thing of faith, or mere belief; and that the severe rebukes and warnings which are contained in the latter portion of it, were the chief occasion of the writer's being stoned to death by the Jewish populace; as that event is supposed to have taken place a short time after the publication of the epistle.

That the encomium of James on good works was intended to explain some of those things in Paul's writings which were hard to be understood, is not improbable; but that it is in direct opposition to them, as some have thought, is not only improbable but impossible. For it is impossible to read Paul's description of charity, in which he declares that it is greater than both faith and hope, and still to believe that he would so directly contradict himself as to reverse this order, and exalt faith above charity; or that he intended by what he calls works, and the works of the law, what we mean by good works and christian morality or virtue. The world have been too long, and much too vehemently disputing about the relative superiority of faith and works, and arraying James against Paul, and Paul against himself. It was, perhaps, a strong bias toward one side of this controversy, or rather a bigoted and dogmatical attachment to it, quite as much as any doubts of the genuineness and antiquity of James' epistle, which induced Luther to call it, in contempt, 'an epistle of straw.' Despite, however, of this coarse epithet of the Reformer, it has maintained its authority in the christian church; an authority, which, if intrinsic excellence and internal evidence have any weight, it amply deserves.

JUDE.

The apostle who stands the tenth on Matthew's list, and is there called 'Lebbeus whose surname was Thaddeus,' is called in Mark's catalogue, 'Thaddeus,' and in Luke's, 'Judas the brother of James.' We cannot fail to remark how carefully he is always distinguished from the other Judas. Matthew and Mark avoid naming him by the name which he held in common with the traitor; and Luke takes care to distinguish him, by adding to that ill omened appellation, that he was the brother of James.

All that is said of him in the sacred histories, *is*, that at the last supper he asked Jesus why he was to manifest himself to his disciples, and not to the world. He was moved to put this question by the views, which, in common with the other disciples, he entertained of the coming of the Messiah; who, as he thought, was to declare himself at last, with great pomp and external power. It was a mystery to him, therefore, how this victorious display was to be made to the small number of his disciples alone, and not to the whole admiring world. The answer of Jesus was not then, in all probability, understood. The meaning and substance of it was, that he and his Father would manifest themselves to those alone, and dwell in those alone, who loved him with that holy love, the fruits of which were righteousness and peace. This strong and beautiful declaration of the spirituality of the Messiah's kingdom, is to be added to those which I have already noticed. The circumstance is related by John in the fourteenth chapter of his Gospel, who designates the apostle as 'Judas, not Iscariot.' No light is any where thrown upon his character; and all that we know of his condition, is, that he was the brother of James the Less, and consequently a cousin of our Lord.

Other accounts of this apostle are so various and contradictory, that it would be wasting time to quote any of them. It is not known with certainty where he preached, or where he died, or whether he died a natural death, or suffered martyrdom. Most of the Latin writers say, that he travelled into Persia, where his labors were very successful, but where, having irritated the Magi by reproving them for their superstitious practices, he was put to a violent death. Some of the Greeks affirm that he died quietly at Berytus; and the Armenians contend that in their country he was martyred.

One epistle has been so generally ascribed to Judas, or Jude, that it has been admitted into the canon of the New Testament. There is hardly another book, however, in that canon, which has been so much disputed. And yet there is no solid reason for rejecting the early tradition, which gives it to this apostle. It was known in the first century, and there is no internal evidence against its apostolic origin.

SIMON ZELOTES.

The next in order is another Simon, who, in the catalogues of Matthew and Mark, is surnamed 'the Canaanite,' and in that of Luke's Gospel, and the book of Acts, 'Zelotes.' Some have thought that the surname, Canaanite, denoted the birthplace of the apostle; but others, with more probability, suppose that Canaanite is merely a Hebrew word, having the same signification with Zelotes, the Greek word used by Luke, and which means a zealot, or one who is extremely zealous. Simon may have received this appellation on account of his having once belonged to a sect or faction among the Jews, who were called Zealots, or only on account of the warmth of his disposition, or the ardor with which he espoused and maintained the cause of Jesus.

It is highly probable, though not certain, that he is the same Simon who is mentioned as one of the brethren or cousins of our Lord. Of the history of his life nothing whatever is known; although the later writers, and martyrologists of the church, pretend, as usual, to be intimately acquainted with it, and give us our choice of a sufficient number of contradictory legends. By some of them, he is made to penetrate as far as Britain, and there to be crucified. By others he is said to have labored in Egypt and Persia, and to have been martyred in the last named country.

JUDAS ISCARIOT.

The last, always the last, on the lists of the apostles, is Judas Iscariot. He is always branded, too, by those fearful and thrilling words, 'who also betrayed him.' And it is sad, that we must close the roll which we have been examining of this glorious apostolic company, with the name of a traitor.

His surname of Iscariot, probably designates his birthplace; as it signifies 'the man of Carioth or Kerioth,' which was a town in the tribe of Judah. But this is hardly more than conjecture. There is a solemn obscurity hanging over the life of this man, shrouding every thing in silent and immoveable shadow; except one deed of gigantic enormity, which raises its high and desert head, and frowns in gloomy solitude over the surrounding waste of darkness and clouds. He is called the son of Simon. Who is Simon? Search the scriptures for him. The search will be vain. He is only known, as has been forcibly said, *only* known by the misfortune of having such a son.

The early dispositions of Judas must have been bad, or he would not have proved himself the wretch that he did, so soon after joining himself to such a Master; and a circumstance recorded in the Gospel of John, plainly intimates to us what the chief vice of his character was. We are informed, that on a visit which Jesus made to Bethany, where Lazarus lived, whom a little while before he had raised from the dead, a supper was made for him there; that Lazarus, with not one trace of death on his countenance, though but just now brought up from the grave, sat at table; and that Martha, with her usual assiduity, served. 'Then took Mary a pound of ointment of spikenard, very costly, and anointed the feet of Jesus, and wiped his feet with her hair; and the house was filled with the odor of the ointment.' This offering, though it may not have been useful, was certainly grateful and generous, and was beside in conformity with the custom of the country, and deserved, therefore, an approving comment from the friends and followers of Jesus. But what was the sequel? 'Then saith one of his disciples, Judas Iscariot, Simon's son, who was to betray him, Why was not this ointment sold for three hundred pence, and given to the poor?' From an honest and really charitable man this remark would have been but a cold one, at such a season; but Judas was neither; and he said this, proceeds the historian, 'not that he cared for the poor, but because he was a thief, and had the bag, and bare off what was put therein.' Thus it appears, that the root of all this traitor's wickedness was avarice, and that it had already borne the deadly fruits of fraud and theft. He had the bag. He had been the treasurer of the fraternity; and so strong was his odious passion, and so weak was his principle, that he was unable to resist the temptation which the trust afforded him, of purloining whatever he could from the common stock, which of necessity must have been a scanty one; and on this occasion he was grievously disappointed, that he could not have the handling of the large sum of three hundred Roman denarii, under the pretence of distributing it to the poor. It is to be presumed that his peculiarities were not known to the apostles at that time, but that they came to light afterwards. If they had then been aware of his conduct, they would doubtless have spurned and avoided him.

Their Master, however, was acquainted both with what he did, and with what he was; for it was on an occasion previous to this, that in reminding the disciples of his own strong claims on their attachment, he said, 'Have not I chosen you twelve? and one of you is a devil!' Here, too, as we are informed, 'he spake of Judas Iscariot, the son of Simon.' And let it be observed, that neither the apostleship of Judas, nor his being the treasurer of the apostles, were causes of his avarice and treachery, and that therefore the knowledge which his Master possessed of his unsoundness is no excuse for it. If he had been a man of common goodness only, the trust which was reposed in him would have prompted him to a worthy exercise of it. Consequently it did not occasion, it only was the means of drawing forth and exposing his baseness. Why our Saviour, acquainted as he was with the character of Judas, permitted him to hold the office of purse bearer; or why he ever called him to be an apostle, are questions of a different import. Before we attempt to assign any reason or motive for the course of Jesus in this respect, let us attend for a moment to its consequences, and its bearing on the credibility of his gospel.

I have already stated, in my introductory remarks, that among the reasons which existed in the mind of our Lord, for calling to himself a company of apostles, one probably was, that his conduct and instructions, being scrutinized by a number of individuals, and continually spread open to their observation, might be sufficiently attested and vindicated, at first to them, and afterwards to the world. This test was made more perfect by the introduction of one among his attendants, whose heart was corrupt, and who would probably turn to as bad account as possible the confidence reposed in him. Thus we see that the inquisition to which the author of our religion was exposed, was a complete one. The honest disciples would have published any thing which they might have seen inconsistent with rectitude; and the traitor, the unprincipled disciple, would have magnified any fault or misconduct in his master, if he could have found any there, as an excuse for his treachery. We ought not to be too hasty in ascribing motives to our Saviour in so grave a concern as this; but with the facts before us, we cannot but feel satisfied that his character rests on a firmer basis from having been thus laid open to the search of a wicked spy, and that his religion derives advantage from the scrutiny. And it is to be repeated, that the apostolic call did not make Judas a thief and a traitor; it found him one already; and if ever any man had the opportunity of reformation offered him, it certainly was he, who daily heard the instructions of heaven, and beheld the example of perfection. We may conclude, therefore, that it was for the satisfaction of all future ages, for our conviction of the faultlessness of Jesus Christ, that Judas was made an apostle.

The answer of our Lord to the covetous remark of his disciple, is narrated as follows. 'Then said Jesus, Let her alone; against the day of my burying hath she kept this. For the poor always ye have with you; but me ye have not always.' That is, 'Suffer this woman to perform her pious work, and molest her not. She is anointing me for my burial; for I know that my hour is at hand, and that the grave is ready for me. Let her alone; it is the last testimony of her gratitude; it is the last mark of affection and reverence which I shall receive on earth; why then should it be called too costly? The claims of the poor are just and strong; I, surely, have never taught you to slight them; but the poor remain with you, and you will have abundant opportunity to relieve them; I am about to depart from you, and go to my Father.'

This rebuke was a mild and touching one; but it affected not the stubborn heart of Judas; it even incited him, perhaps, to execute immediately his before conceived purpose of betraying his Master into the hands of his enemies; for very soon after it had been uttered, he went unto the chief priests, and bargained with them to deliver up Jesus into their power, for thirty pieces of silver; a sum not more than about a third of what the ointment had cost; and from that time he sought opportunity to betray him.

It has been a subject of great surprise with many commentators, that so small a bribe should have tempted Judas to commit so great a crime; and it does seem as if some other motive must have cooperated with the love of money, in bringing his mind to its dreadful determination. Among the solutions which have been proposed of this apparent enigma, is the one which supposes that Judas was impatient of the delay of his Master to assume the state and magnificence of his Messiahship, and that his intention was to compel him to do so, by bringing him into such imminent peril, that he would be obliged to call his followers round him, work some signal miracle to free himself, and then mount the throne of David and of Israel. In this event, he of course calculated that he should come in for his share of those offices and rewards which he had been long pining for, and pining for in vain. Here, also, avarice is the governing motive; only on a much larger scale than in the action as it is simply narrated in the scriptures.

There is something to say in favor of this explanation, and something too may be said against it. It is safest and easiest to take the bare gospel statement, which merely informs us, that, for the consideration of thirty shekels of silver, Judas covenanted to betray his Master. No motive is expressly assigned for the act; but as he is represented as selfish and avaricious, we must presume that selfishness and avarice moved him to this last and most awful crime. With regard to the price of his treachery, a survey of human nature and human passions will not authorise us to say that any sum is too small to tempt habitual and absorbing avarice to any act or degree of wickedness. Earthly, sensual, and contemptible, there is no knowing how low this passion will creep, nor how high it will strike; how meanly it may dig for its dirty food, nor how daringly it may direct its poison.

Having concluded his bargain with the priests, and as he thought secretly, Judas resumed his place among the twelve, and the next that we hear of him is at the last supper. As they were eating, Jesus said, 'Verily I say unto you, that one of you shall betray me.' At this intimation, the disciples, innocent as they all but one, felt themselves to be, were exceedingly distressed, and they began each one to say unto him, 'Lord, is it I?' Jesus, who had just before discovered the traitor, by a sign, to Simon Peter and John, answered, and said, 'He that dippeth his hand with me in the dish, the same shall betray me. The Son of Man goeth, as it is written of him; but wo unto that man by whom the son of man is betrayed! it had been good for that man if he had not been born.' Judas, who, in all probability, saw that his Master's hand and his own were together in the dish, and that he was consequently accused of the treason, but still, perhaps, relying on the secrecy with which he had made his bargain, thought that he now was obliged to say something; and pretending the same innocence as the rest, he asked the same question, 'Lord, is it I?' And Jesus using no more signs, but directly accusing the miserable culprit, answered, 'Thou hast said.' He then added, 'That which thou doest, do quickly.' Judas, finding that no disguise or equivocation would now serve him, went immediately out. 'And it was night,' adds the historian. Night indeed! How dark, how thick, how suffocating! There never was another such since the world first woke from chaos. We seem to see it fall and settle like an outstretched pall, and closely gather in and embrace the whole of that devoted region with its black and muffled folds. Under its covering the wretched apostle stole forth to execute his purpose; what a night there must have been in his bosom, and in his mind! And what a night, of doubt and fear and mournfulness, did he leave in the hearts of the eleven, who now listened sadly to their Master, as he pursued his melting, though calm, sustained, and heavenly discourse, and gave them his farewell exhortations, and his farewell blessing!

It was yet night, when the small company, now made smaller by desertion, having finished their supper and sung a hymn together, went out, as was the frequent custom of Jesus, to the mount of Olives. Here he suffered his dreadful agony; and here Judas soon appeared, with an armed band, which he had received from the priests and Pharisees; for he knew that he should probably find his Master in this place of his usual resort. In order that his attendants might be sure of their victim, in this season of confusion and darkness, the traitor gave them a sign, telling them that whomsoever he should kiss, the same was he. Then going up to Jesus, as if he had been a friend, and intended to offer the common salutation of friendship and intimacy, he said, 'Hail Master!' and kissed him. Reproachfully Jesus said unto him, 'Judas, betrayest thou the Son of Man with a kiss?' 'Is it with a hypocritical kiss of affection and peace that you perform this deed of atrocious ingratitude?' Then Jesus said unto the chief priests, and captains of the temple, and the elders, who were come to him, 'Be ye come out, as against a thief, with swords and staves? When I was daily with you in the temple, ye stretched forth no hands against me; but this is your hour, and the power of darkness.' Then they took him and brought him to the high priest's house.

And now that Judas has accomplished his design, is he gratified? At first perhaps he was. But it was a momentary satisfaction. Reflection succeeded passion, and grief and remorse followed hard upon the footsteps of reflection. He could think now; and he could feel. He could think how good his Master had always been to him; how perfectly free from guilt or stain, and yet how condescending and pitiful to human error. He felt the baseness of his own conduct; he was appalled at the sight of his own enormous ingratitude; he began to hate himself, and to fear the light of morning, and to dread the aspect of that mild face, which however mildly it might regard him, could speak nothing to his heart but judgment and agony. Morning came. The relentless and exulting enemies of Jesus met to adopt measures for securing their prey. As the fate of his Master approached nearer to its bloody catastrophe, the anguish of Judas became more intense, and his crime showed itself in all its horrors. Perhaps he did not apprehend that the priests would have pushed their malignity to the extreme of death. At any rate, his own malice and cupidity were wholly terrified away, and he resolved to make one wild effort to save the victim. He rushed to the conclave, with the now hateful silver grasped convulsively in his hand, and reaching it out to his employers, he exclaimed, 'I have sinned, in that I have betrayed innocent blood.' Deluded man! Innocent or guilty it was the same to them, so long as they could destroy him. 'And they said, What is that to us? See thou to that!' Stung to the quick by this cold and insulting reply, and feeling himself cast away like a tool which has been broken in the using, and having now no refuge from the fiends that were pursuing him, existence became a burthen too heavy for him to bear; and he threw the pieces of silver on the pavement of the temple, 'and departed, and went and hanged himself.'

I know not how others may feel on perusing the history of this wretched man, but for my own part, I confess that my indignation is plentifully mingled with pity. How dark was the close of his short career! How terrible was the punishment of his guilt; death by his own hands! The price of blood lies scattered at the feet of the priests; the betrayer has come to his end, even before the betrayed; his apostleship is ended; no softened multitude will listen to the tidings of salvation from his lips; no converts to a pure and purifying faith will bow to receive the waters of baptism from his hands; no countries will contend for the honor of his grave; no churches will call themselves by his name; no careful disciples compose his limbs; no enthusiastic devotees gather up his bones; his dust is scattered to the winds; his name is only preserved by its eternal ignominy. He was a martyr—the first martyr—but it was to avarice. He has had his followers, too; but they have been only those, who, as wicked and as wretched as himself, have, from that day to this, and in the countless forms of selfishness, sold, for a few pieces of silver, their consciences, their Saviour, and their souls.

By an observable coincidence, it so happened that the money which Judas had received and returned, became desecrated by his touch. There was a Jewish law, which forbade that the price of blood should be put into the treasury. The priests, therefore, though they gathered up the pieces which the traitor had thrown down before them, were unable to appropriate them to the uses of the temple, and after consulting together, agreed to purchase with them a field in the vicinity of Jerusalem, called the Potter's Field, to bury strangers in. The piece of ground thus purchased, acquired the significant and fearful name of *The Field of Blood*.

When the tragedy of the crucifixion was over, and the eleven, comforted and reassured by the appearance of their risen Lord, had assembled together in Jerusalem, with the other disciples, to the number of about an hundred and twenty, Peter proposed to the company that a disciple should be chosen by lot to take ' the ministry and apostleship, from which Judas, by transgression, fell.' In the address which he made on this occasion, he gives an account of the death of Judas, which differs somewhat from the relation of Matthew. 'Now this man,' he says, 'purchased a field with the reward of iniquity; and falling headlong, he burst asunder in the midst, and all his bowels gushed out.' Several explanations have been given to reconcile this discrepancy, either of which is sufficiently probable to answer the purpose. The most common one is, that Judas hung himself, as Matthew relates, and afterwards, by some accident, fell from the place where he was suspended, and was mangled in the shocking manner described by Peter.

According to the apostle's recommendation, his brethren proceeded to fill the traitor's forfeited place; and the lot fell upon Matthias, who had long been a disciple of Jesus, and is conjectured to have been one of the seventy. Thus was the miserable Judas, the apostate, the suicide, rejected from the apostolic company, even after his death, and his name and his memory blotted out, as entirely as was possible, from the records of the faithful. With the passage of scripture which were applied on this occasion by Peter, we will conclude his mournful biography. 'For it is written in the book of Psalms, Let his habitation be desolate, and let no man dwell therein; and his bishopric let another take.'

CONCLUDING REMARKS.

The lives and characters of the twelve apostles of Christ have now been separately considered; but there are some general reflections upon them, regarded collectively, which naturally suggested themselves during the course that we have been through, and which may not prove uninteresting or uninstructive to those who have accompanied me in the way.

We find, with respect to the circumstances of their external condition—their country, their fortunes, their education—that they were such as most readily presented themselves to the search of Jesus, and yet not such, by any means, as we should suppose would have been effective in the accomplishment of his designs.

In the first place, the apostles were all Galileans; natives or inhabitants of the district of Galilee. This country constituted the northern portion of Palestine, and its people, though hardy and brave, were not much respected by the Jews of Jerusalem, who regarded them as illiterate and unpolished, and unworthy of producing a prophet. The Pharisees, reproving Nicodemus for the interest which he expressed in Jesus, said to him, tauntingly, 'Art thou also of Galilee? Search, and look; for out of Galilee ariseth no prophet.' The very speech of the Galileans was a provincial dialect, and betrayed their remoteness from the capital; as we have seen was the case with Peter in the palace of Caiaphas. In short they were looked down upon by the more cultivated, and, if I may use the epithet, *Attic* part of the nation, as a rude, unenlightened, Bœotian branch of the common Jewish family. Jesus, though born in Bethlehem, was brought up in Nazareth, which was the most despised town in this most despised province; and therefore in selecting Galileans to be his apostles, he selected those who were nearest to him, and with whom he was most familiar. And yet what materials were they for constructing and building up a new religion, which was to be the wonder, the beauty, and the glory of the earth! How little adapted they seem to be for their lofty destination! They are the last men, these poor Galileans, the very last men, as we should suppose, to confound the learned, to resist the mighty, to convert the world. They do not seem to be made for such a work. There is no fitness in them to be instructers and reformers. Their very birthplace forbids it. The choice of them, therefore, to be the intimate disciples of Christ, and the founders of a new religious system, appears to me to be a mark of the divine mission of Christ, and the divine character and origin of Christianity. To my ear the language of it is this; The person, who, undertaking to introduce a peculiar and original faith to the world, selected, or, as it would rather appear, took almost carelessly up, his associates and confidential coadjutors, from his own neighbourhood, from his own kindred, from the shores of a lake, from the streets of a village, from before his own doorstone, instead of seeking out the learned and the powerful from among the Pharisees and chief men of the nation, must have set out in his work with the assurance that there was a Power and a Wisdom above, which could and would supply every deficiency among his followers; and the event proved that the deficiency *was* supplied from a divine, all sufficient, and only sufficient Source.

These Galileans were also poor. Four of them were certainly fishermen; and others of their number were probably of the same profession. One was a publican, and of the inferior order of publicans. They not only belonged to an undervalued province, but they were destitute of one of those means by which great ends are usually produced in the world. They were not, indeed, wretchedly destitute. They were above actual want, though they worked for their living; and their dwellings, though humble, appear to have been comfortable. But they were far from being rich; far from possessing any of that influence and consequence which wealth so universally commands. And yet without wealth, they effected what no wealth could have brought to pass; and became of more consequence than ever invests princes.

Beside these disadvantages, they were also unlearned. I do not mean that they were rudely ignorant, or that they were unacquainted with the sacred literature of their nation; but they were neither deeply versed in lore, nor elegantly accomplished. They could not take a place among the well educated portion of their countrymen. Their manner of expressing themselves at once betrayed this kind and degree of ignorance to those who were more polished and better instructed. Thus the council of elders and rulers before which Peter and John were arraigned, perceived that those apostles were 'unlearned and ignorant men.' And yet they were not so unlearned and ignorant that they did not, both of them, give to the church, and to the world, writings in the Greek language, which, though not exactly classical, were by no means despicable, even in their style. But their speech, provincial and uncultivated as it was, sent conviction to the hearts of multitudes; and their writings, simple and unpolished as they were, threw a new and heavenly radiance over that dark world, have instructed ages and generations, and impart more real knowledge on the highest objects of thought, than the greatest philosophers of antiquity had ever been able to impart. To my mind this is a remarkable fact; and one which does not easily admit of but one explanation.

We may sum up the circumstances of the external condition of the apostles, by saying, that they were what would now be called plain, substantial men, in the lower walks of life. They were in a situation, not exceedingly depressed, and yet more remarkable for its humility than otherwise. Their education was only such a one as was usually bestowed on the common people of their nation, and in all probability consisted chiefly in a knowledge of the scriptures of the Old Testament, which scriptures they interpreted according to the instructions of the Rabbis, and the general expectations, opinions, and prejudices of their countrymen.

With regard to their natural dispositions, talents, and endowments of mind, there was among them the same assortment and variety of genius and character as would generally be found in the same number of men called together in a similar manner. Peter was irrascible, impetuous, fervent, generous. John was amiable, affectionate, steadfast. Thomas was honest and scrutinizing. Matthew was modest and sensible. James the Greater was active and aspiring. James the Less was dignified in his sentiments and deportment. Some were forward, and some were retired. Some were eloquent, and others were silent. All, but one, appear to have been virtuous; and even that one was not without his use. They all, with that single exception, combined harmoniously in attachment to their Master and devotion to his cause. We may see in this fact, that Christianity was adapted to different dispositions, and received by different minds; that it was not merely the enthusiastic who accepted and supported it; that it was judged by different tests; that it was regarded through various optics; that zeal embraced it; that cool sense approved it; that candor and honesty were convinced by it; that even disappointed avarice could report nothing against it. We see too in this fact, an instance of the truth, which is at once so obvious and so little regarded, that a variety of genius and disposition is in accordance with the designs of Providence in its most important operations with human instruments, as well as in the daily and social business of the world; and that a character is by no means to be despised because its qualities are not shining and striking. There are different parts to be performed, requiring different powers and capacities; and he who achieves his part, though it be a silent and undistinguished one, is a good servant.

We are told much, in the writings of the New Testament, of the words and actions of Simon Peter; but little or nothing of those of Simon Zelotes and Bartholomew; and yet these latter may have accomplished tasks which were necessary to the progress of the great work, but which would not have suited the peculiar capacity of Peter. They may have reached minds which he could not touch; they may have performed duties, subordinate indeed, but still necessary, such as he was not gifted to perform. Each apostle takes his own place, and stands easily and naturally in it; neither stretching after what was above, nor contemning what was below him. In this instance, as well as in others, we may derive a lesson from them.

In another point of view, the company of the apostles presents us with a spectacle, which, though it may not be a very instructive, is certainly a pleasing one. Within their common fraternity there were no less than three distinct bands of natural brethren. Peter and Andrew were brothers; John and James the Greater were brothers; and so also were James the Less, Jude or Thaddeus, and Simon Zelotes. With the ties of a common faith, of a common toil, and a common danger, were thus beautifully blended the ties of consanguinity and domestic affection; and a texture of harmonious coloring was completed in this companionship, such as is seldom woven on earth. The three brethren last named were also near relations of Jesus himself. The reflections which are readily suggested by this circumstance, are, that our Saviour was beloved at home as well as abroad; and that the familiarity of relationship did not impair the respect in which he was held as a master and teacher. We see also in this fact, another cause of his love for his disciples, and of their love for him; a cause which is far from diminishing our reverence for him, or our interest in them. They were not strangers to each other; they were not brought together merely by the attractions of sympathy, or the demands of a great work. They were not countrymen only; they were neighbours, partners, early acquaintances;—they were more, for they were kinsmen, with the mutual attachments of kindred; and they go about on their labors before us, a more social, united, confidential, and interesting group, than if there had been no family bonds to strengthen and adorn their union.

Let us next view the apostles as authors, and as subjects of history. I should wonder at the state of that man's affections who could read the Gospels, two of which were written by apostles, without being struck by the exceeding modesty and selfforgetfulness of the disciples, and their absorbing attention to one individual, their venerated and beloved Master.

There are no vaunts in those sacred histories; no instances of open or disguised egotism. When the writer speaks of his fellow disciples, he relates with the utmost simplicity their faults, and prejudices, and want of faith, as well as the better parts of their characters. And he speaks of his Master, too, with equal simplicity, but with how much greater frequency and devotion! He brings every other person, every other thing, he brings himself under perfect subordination to this main subject of his narrative. He does this, not artfully and intentionally, but unavoidably; from feeling, from impulse, from the conviction that there is but one individual of whom he is giving an account; and if others are mentioned, they are mentioned because they are in some manner connected with that person. If Jesus has occasion to praise one of his disciples, the evangelist records the fact without envy; if that disciple, or any other one is rebuked, he relates it without evasion or excuse. He keeps himself to the sayings and actions of his Master, as to his chief concern. He indulges in no inferences, no moral reflections, no expression of his own views or feelings; he writes pure history, simple narrative; and on all occasions he tells, without reserve and without suspicion, the plain truth; we see and feel that he does; there is an honesty about every relation which cannot be mistaken or suspected. And we see and feel, too, that the chief personage of the history is not brought out into such entire relief, into such a concentration of light, by any effort or design on the part of the writer, but only and wholly on account of the unapproached sublimity and intrinsic superiority of the character itself.

There is one other circumstance in the lives of the apostles, which I am bound to notice for the sake of its singularity and importance; and then I will leave them to the meditations and further inquiries of my readers. I have several times had occasion to speak of the national prejudices of these men, and the difficulty which they had to comprehend the entire spirituality of their Master's system and kingdom, and to admit into their associations with the Jewish Messiah and Saviour the ideas of poverty, lowliness, suffering, and death. Attached as they were to him by all the ties which we have enumerated, we see that when he was actually apprehended by his enemies, they all forsook him and fled; that they did not return to him; and that on the Mount where he was crucified, there was but one of them who appeared to witness the death of their Master and kinsman, and the extinction of all their hopes. The event was one for which they were wholly unprepared. It confounded them. Their preconceived opinions were so strong, that when Jesus had before spoken to them of his death, they shut up their ears and their eyes, they *would not* understand him. We do not find a single hint in the Gospels, that they ever did understand him. The event itself was a blow, which at once enlightened and convinced them, and scattered them abroad also, like sheep without a shepherd. This is one scene.

And now let us behold another, which immediately succeeds it. Not a great many days elapse, when we find these very men, disheartened, disappointed, terrified, and dispersed as they had been, all gathered together again with one accord, fully recovered from all their depression, and with a settled resolution stamped on all their demeanour, which never marked them before, even while their Master was with them, to lead, combine, and encourage them. The catalogue of their names is full, with one vacancy only, which they immediately supply. They begin to preach the doctrines of a crucified Saviour, and we hear no more of their earthly notions of his kingdom. Their crude ideas and temporal hopes have, in a few days, vanished away. They preach Christianity, simply and purely. They gather to themselves thousands of converts. They are persecuted, imprisoned, threatened; they behold one of their number soon cut off with the sword; they are surrounded by enemies and temptations; and yet they never hesitate nor falter; no, not the weakest of them; there is not a single defection from their reunited brotherhood. They go through country after country, and toil after toil, laying down their lives, one after another, for the holy truth, and they leave disciples behind them everywhere, to teach, and dare, and suffer, and do, and die, as they did.

Now what is the cause of all this, and how is it to be accounted for? Unbelievers may have many explanations to give, and they may be ingenious ones. I have but one, and it is a simple one. It is, that their crucified Master rose from the dead, as they have told us he did; that he instructed them, as they have told us he did; and that the Holy Spirit, the Comforter, was sent from the Father, according to his promise, to enlighten and sustain them. In short, I consider the conduct of the apostles, at, and after the death of Jesus, as perhaps the strongest proof of the reality of his glorious resurrection. If he rose from the dead, and appeared to them, and instructed and confirmed them, I can account for the sudden change in their characters, and for their subsequent knowledge and perseverance, and boldness, and success. If he rose not from the dead, I cannot account for those things; and the whole subject remains to me a deep historical mystery.

Simple, honest, excellent men! raised up by Providence for wonderful ends by wonderful means! Your lives, unadorned as they are, and comprehended in a few plain words, are yet alone among the lives of men; alone, in the varieties and contrasts of their fortunes; alone, in the multitude and importance of their consequences. We should be senseless, if we did not perceive the influence which you have exerted on the character and opinions of mankind. We should be thankless, if we did not acknowledge the benefits of that influence, and bless God that we live to know and feel them. And we humbly pray to God, the universal Father, the Source of all excellence and truth, that our fidelity to our common Master may be like yours; that our perseverance in executing his commands may be like yours; and that like yours may be our courage and constancy, if we should ever be called on to sacrifice comfort, worldly consideration, or life itself, to duty, conscience, and faith.

NOTES.

NOTES.

NOTES TO THE INTRODUCTION.

Page 5. We are also presented with a similar catalogue in the Gospels of Mark, &c.

For facility of reference, the three remaining lists of the twelve are here subjoined.

'And Simon he surnamed Peter; and James the son of Zebedee; and John the brother of James; and he surnamed them Boanerges, which is, The Sons of Thunder; and Andrew; and Philip; and Bartholomew; and Matthew; and Thomas; and James the son of Alpheus; and Thaddeus; and Simon the Canaanite; and Judas Iscariot, who also betrayed him.' *Mark*, iii. 16, 17, 18, 19.

'Simon, whom he also named Peter; and Andrew his brother; James and John; Philip and Bartholomew; Matthew and Thomas; James the son of Alpheus, and Simon called Zelotes; and Judas the brother of James, and Judas Iscariot who also was the traitor.' *Luke*, vi. 14, 15, 16.

'Peter, and James, and John, and Andrew, Philip and Thomas, Bartholomew, and Matthew, James the son of Alpheus, and Simon Zelotes, and Judas the brother of James.' *Acts*, i. 13.

Page 5. *Why the exact number of twelve, &c.*

The conjectures of the Fathers, on this subject, are fanciful, and endless. There was most probably a reference to the twelve tribes in the number of the apostles; over which tribes they were to exercise spiritual authority, in the day of their Master's glory.

NOTES TO THE LIFE OF PETER.

Page 16. *Otherwise called the Sea of Tiberias, &c.*

This lake took its name of *Galilee* from the province in which it was situated, and of *Genesareth* and *Tiberias*, from towns on its coasts.

Page 29. *By and by, and from another quarter, he is again attacked with the same charge.*

There are some apparent discrepances in the several accounts given by the evangelists of Peter's denial of his Master. But they are only apparent; and indeed the veracity of the sacred writers is rather confirmed by these slight differences, which ought to be expected in separate narratives of what must necessarily have been a confused and hurried scene. John, for instance, says that Peter *stood* with the officers at the fire, and Matthew and Mark say that he *sat*. Doubtless he sat at one time and stood at another, in the agitation he was in, and therefore both relations are not only true, but more strikingly authentic from their very appearance of discrepancy. Again, there is a difference with regard to the persons who are represented as having at several times accused Peter. Now, it is highly probable that though the apostle made but three distinct denials, he was yet accused by many, who in a tumultuous manner may have raised their voices against him, and thus rendered it doubtful who was the prominent assailant among a number of clamorous witnesses. In short, the accounts of the evangelists are evidently but sketches of a scene in which many things occurred which are not related by either, and some things, which are recorded by one, though omitted by another. The main facts, however, agree in all; and this being the case, the variations accord so well with the character of the scene described, and the agitation which all parties must have been in, that they only add truth to truth.

It will be observed, that in these Lives I do not often name the evangelist, or the chapter and verse, from which I make my quotations. The reason of the omission was, that I should have been obliged to insert so many references, that the narrative would have been interrupted and the page deformed, without any advantage arising from such a method, important enough to counterbalance those evils. Any particular passage, or portion of the narrative, can easily be verified by turning to the bible.

Page 32. *Who, by his shadow alone, healed many who were laid in his way.*

It is not expressly asserted in Acts, v. 15, that those persons were healed by Peter's shadow, and therefore some commentators have taken it for granted that they were not, and have even gone so far as to assert that the apostle's neglect of them was a punishment for their superstition. So says Rosenmuller. But in the next verse we are told that great numbers of sick persons were also brought to him from the cities round about, and 'were healed every one.' Now there seems to be no good reason why these should be healed, and those who belonged to the city should be neglected. Their being placed in

Peter's way, so that even his shadow might pass over them, shows more the affectionate and confident faith of them and their friends, than it does their superstition. If Peter was empowered from on high to heal diseases, he could do so by his shadow, as well as by a touch or a few words. His will was the agent; the signs of its exertion were of no importance in themselves. As we are not informed that Peter rebuked those who laid the sick under his shadow, the most reasonable and compassionate inference is, that these, as well as the others, were healed.

Page 33. *Tabitha, or Dorcas.*
Tabitha being the Syriac name, and Dorcas its translation into Greek. They both mean a kid or goat.

Page 35. *When Peter was come to Antioch.*
Ecclesiastical historians say that Peter founded the church at Antioch, and some add that he was its first bishop.

Page 36. *He is said to have been bishop of Rome for twentyfour or twentyfive years.*
This is denied by the learned Cave, in his Life of this apostle, who contends that the authority for such a length of time is insufficient, and that Peter probably spent but a few years at Rome before his death, St Paul being there at the same time, and governing the church jointly with him. He also inclines to the opinion that neither Peter nor Paul was, properly speaking, bishop of the Roman church, but by their united exertions they planted it, and that its first bishop was Linus, who, by the Catholics, is placed next to St Peter in the episcopal see. The truth is, that while the Catholics endeavour to show that Peter favored the great city with the most of his time, and

was the first who sat on the chair afterwards occupied by the popes, the Protestants are interested to dispute every step of the process, and, on account of the looseness of ancient ecclesiastical history, find it easy to do so.

One of the most remarkable passages of Peter's life at Rome, according to the Fathers, was a desperate contention with his old enemy, Simon Magus, whom at last, by miracles and prayers, he entirely defeated.

Cave calculates that the apostle was crucified in the time of Nero's persecution of the Christians, after the burning of Rome, and in about the year 64 of the christian era. The day appropriated to him in the Roman Calendar of Saints, is June 29.

The following description of his person is from the Ecclesiastical History of Nicephorus. We may look on it as a curiosity, if not a true portrait. 'His body was somewhat slender, of a middle size, but rather inclining to tallness; his complexion very pale and almost white; the hair of his head and beard curled and thick, but withal short; though St Jerome tells us that he was bald, which probably might be in his declining age; his eyes black, but specked with red; his eyebrows thin, or none at all; his nose long, but rather broad and flat than sharp.'

Page 36. *It is probable that he was a married man.*

That he was married when he was called to be an apostle, is certain, as the scriptures mention his 'wife's mother.' But staunch Catholics, with Jerome at their head, will have it, that he left his wife when he left all to follow Jesus. This, however, does not well agree with the testimony of Paul. Clemens Alexandrinus relates, that Peter, seeing his wife going to be martyred, exceedingly rejoiced that she was elected to so great an honor, and that she was now returning home, and calling her by her name, encouraged and exhorted her, bidding her to be mindful of our Lord. The apostle is also said to have had a daughter, by the name of Petronilla.

NOTES TO THE LIFE OF ANDREW.

Page 39. *And thus made himself his first disciple.*

Andrew is generally styled by the ancient writers of the church, *Protocletos*, or *the first called*. The following encomium on him, is by Hesychius, Presbyter of Jerusalem. 'St Andrew was the first born of the Apostolic Choir; the prime pillar of the church; a rock before the rock; the foundation of that foundation; the first fruits of the beginning; a caller of others before he was called himself. He preached that gospel which was not yet believed or entertained; revealed and made known that life to his brother, which he had not yet perfectly learned himself. So great treasures did that one question bring him, "Master, where dwellest thou?" which he soon perceived by the answer given him, and which he deeply pondered in his mind, "Come, and see."'

Page 41. *He preached the gospel in various countries.*

Scythia, various provinces of Greece, and Byzantium, or Constantinople, are particularly mentioned as the scenes of his labors. At Sinope, on the Euxine Sea, he is said to have met with his brother Peter.

Page 41. *Was at last crucified.*

On approaching the cross to which he was condemned to be bound with cords, that his death might be more lingering, he is said, by one of the ancients, to have apostrophized it in the following ardent manner;—'Hail, precious cross, which has been consecrated by the body of my Lord! how ardently have I loved thee! how long have I sought thee! at length I have found thee, now waiting to receive my longing soul. Take and snatch me from among mortals and present me to my Master, that he who redeemed me on thee, may receive me at thy hands.'

The instrument of his martyrdom is commonly affirmed to have been what is called a *cross decussate,* made by two pieces of timber crossing each other in the middle, in the form of the letter X, and hence known by the name of St Andrew's Cross.

Andrew is the patron Saint of Scotland. The day consecrated to him in the Calendar is November 30.

NOTES TO THE LIFE OF JAMES THE GREATER.

Page 49. *And he killed James, the brother of John, with the sword.*

This Herod was Herod Agrippa, the grandson of Herod the Great, in whose reign Christ was born. He was a distinguished favorite of the Roman emperors, Caligula and his successor Claudius, though a strict and zealous observer of the Jewish law. On entering upon his government he was desirous of doing something to please the Jewish populace, and for that end began to persecute the infant christian church, selecting for a principal victim, James the brother of John. We are informed by Clemens Alexandrinus, that as the apostle was led forth to the place of execution, the person who had accused him was so touched with the courage and constancy which he displayed, that he repented of what he had done, came and fell down at his feet, and earnestly begged pardon for what he had said against him. St James tenderly raised him up, kissed him, and said to him, 'Peace be to thee, my son, and the pardon of thy faults.' At this, his former accuser publicly professed himself a Christian, and so both were beheaded at the same time. Not long after this martyrdom, Herod suffered a miserable death, as is related in Acts, xii. 23., and more at large by Josephus in the nineteenth book of his Antiquities.

Page 49. *He was the first of the apostles who suffered martyrdom.*

He is therefore called the Apostolic Protomartyr; Stephen being the Protomartyr, or first martyr, of the whole christian church. He is the James who is called by the Spaniards St James of Compostella, and honored as their patron Saint. They receive with general faith a wild and singular legend, which gives an account of the manner in which they became possessed of his remains. According to this story, the apostles at Jerusalem sent the body in a vessel with Ctesiphon, whom they ordained bishop of Spain. The vessel went directly to a port in that kingdom, without the assistance of oars or pilot, guided only by its holy, though lifeless burthen, which, on its arrival, was miraculously taken away and buried, and after a great many wonders, was at last translated to Compostella, where it stills abides, the object of constant pilgrimage, and the worker of countless miracles. Cave, after giving this legend rather more at length, observes;— 'This is the sum of the account, call it romance or history, which I do not desire to impose any further upon the reader's faith than he shall find himself disposed to believe it.'

Ferdinand II. of Spain instituted a *military* order in honor of this apostle. His festival is on the 26th of July.

NOTES TO THE LIFE OF JOHN.

Page 52. *Went with Peter to the palace of the high priest, and gained him admittance there by means of his acquaintance with that dignitary.*

'That disciple was known unto the high priest.' John, xviii. 15. The early writers busy themselves to find out in what manner John became acquainted with Caiaphas. Jerome says that he belonged to some order of nobility; which, however, seems to be very inconsistent with the occupation of his father. Nicephorus relates, that he sold his paternal estate in Galilee to the high priest, and with the money purchased a fair house in Jerusalem, and so became intimate with him. These stories seem to me, like many other similar ones, to prove two things; one, that the early christian writers were exceedingly anxious to explain the slightest hints in the gospel histories; the other, that they were much too apt to write down the first report which came to their ears, glad to catch something, and not careful to sift the truth. Hence the contradictory statements with which their works are full.

Page 53. *Four weeping females.*

They were Mary the mother of Jesus, Mary Magdalene, Mary the mother of James the Less and of Joses, and Salome the mother of James the Greater and of

John. There were other women in company with them, but these four probably stood nearer the cross than the rest.

Page 58. *And others again assert that his life was protracted beyond that term.*

So respectable a writer as Chrysostom asserts, in one of his sermons, that John was an hundred years old when he wrote his Gospel, and that he lived twenty years afterwards. But this is worthy of but little credit. Again, many of the ancients entertained the absurd belief that this apostle never died, but was translated like Enoch and Elias.

Page 58. *The affectionate mildness of his character.*

All the ancient testimonies concur on the subject of the gentleness of this apostle. One of the best authenticated stories of his latter days, is, as related by Jerome, that when age and weakness grew upon him at Ephesus, so that he was no longer able to preach to his converts, he used, at every public meeting, to be led to the church, and say no more to them than these words, 'Little children, love one another.' And when his auditors, wearied with the constant repetition of the same thing, asked him why he always said this and nothing more to them, he answered, 'Because it was the command of our Lord, and that if they did nothing else, this alone was enough.'

Page 59. *The book of the Revelation.*

I call it so, because it is so called in the bible; though the more common title is, the book of Revelations.

Page 60. *The poet Milton.*

That Milton understood the Apocalypse to be a general prophecy, in the form of a religious drama, I gather from the following passage in his *Reason of Church Government urged against Prelaty*. 'And the Apocalypse of St John is the majestic image of a high and stately tragedy, shutting up and intermingling her solemn scenes and acts with a sevenfold chorus of hallelujahs and harping symphonies; and this my opinion, the grave authority Pareus, commenting that book, is sufficient to confirm.'

Page 62. *The Disciple whom Jesus loved.*

The ancients also called him *The Divine*, on account of the sublimity and spirituality of his writings.

His festival is December 27, in the Roman Calendar; but the Greeks keep it on the 26th of September.

NOTES TO THE LIFE OF PHILIP.

Page 63. *And saith unto him, Follow me.*

Though Peter and Andrew were the first who appear to have attended on the instructions of Jesus, and to have been particularly noticed by him, and are therefore called his first disciples, yet it is to Philip that the distinction belongs of having been first called to be a companion and *apostle* of Christ.

Page 65. *That he preached in Phrygia, and that he was buried at Hieropolis.*

Hieropolis was a city of Phrygia, very much given to idolatry; and it was by causing an object of superstitious worship to be destroyed, that Philip is said to have incurred his death there, which was inflicted by hanging him by his neck to a pillar. The Roman Catholics keep his festival on the 1st of May.

NOTES TO THE LIFE OF BARTHOLOMEW.

Page 68. *In the Indies, in Arabia, and Persia.*

He is also said to have preached in Phrygia, at the same time with Philip, and to have narrowly escaped death when his fellow apostle was martyred.

Page 68. *Died in Albana.*

His body is believed by the Catholics to be now deposited in a porphyry monument under the high altar of the church of St Bartholomew in Rome. August 24th is observed as his festival.

NOTES TO THE LIFE OF THOMAS.

Page 76. *He travelled through many parts of the Indies.*

Of this general fact there is little doubt; and it is said that a community of Christians, still existing in the East, own St Thomas as their founder.

Page 76. *He suffered martyrdom.*

He is stated to have been run through the body with a lance, by a Brachman, while he was at his devotions. This took place at Malipur, or Meliapor, on the coast of Coromandel, where he had made many converts, among whom was the king of the country, and where he had built a church. In this church he was buried, as those tell us who deny that his body was carried to Edessa in Mesopotamia; and in this church they say the following miracle was to be witnessed at all times. A lamp hangs before his tomb, which burns perpetually, needing no oil, and undisturbed in its flame by the wind or any accident whatever. This is one of those legends, which, though deserving no more credit than others of the same class, is beautiful in itself, and highly pleasing to the imagination.

The 21st of December is devoted to this apostle, in the Roman Calendar.

NOTES TO THE LIFE OF MATTHEW.

Page 80. *At the receipt of custom.*

It appears from the relation of Mark, in the second chapter of his Gospel, that Matthew's official station was at the seaside, where he was sitting when Jesus called him. Commentators say that the particular duty of Matthew as a publican, was to gather the customs of commodities which came by the Sea of Galilee, and the tribute which passengers were to pay who went by water. According to this statement, he was a tollgatherer.

Page 83. *Matthew is said to have carried the religion of Jesus into Parthia, and Ethiopia, &c.*

'Little certainty can be had,' says Cave, 'what travels he underwent for the advancement of the christian faith, so irrecoverably is truth lost in a crowd of legendary stories. Ethiopia is generally assigned as the province of his apostolical ministry.' His festival, according to the Roman Calendar, is on the 21st of September. It may here be observed that the Roman and Greek Calendars differ from each other in their dates, from beginning to end.

NOTES TO THE LIFE OF JAMES THE LESS.

Page 86. *He is consequently our Lord's cousin.*

The exact relationship to Jesus of James the Less, and others, who are called his brethren, was a matter of controversy in very early times. Respectable names appear on each side; and Cave says that a majority of the ancients were of opinion that these 'brethren' were actually the sons of Joseph by a former wife. It has appeared to me that the other opinion is the most likely to be the true one, and I have therefore called James the cousin of Jesus. One of the strongest arguments for this view of the relationship, is, that the father of James is called Alpheus, and not Joseph, and that Mary the wife of Cleophas is mentioned in the Gospel of John as a person entirely distinct from the mother of Jesus, and further appears to be the same who is called by Mark the mother of James the Less and of Joses. Now Alpheus and Cleophas being the same name, the chain of testimony is complete; so complete, that I wonder any question should ever have been raised on the subject.

Page 91. *Eight or ten years before the destruction of Jerusalem.*

So great was the reputation of James for sanctity, that his death was supposed by the Jews themselves to have hastened the destruction of their city. Some of the Fathers tell us that this was asserted by Josephus; but the passage is not now to be found in his works. Both the accounts of James's death agree that he was stoned. It is added in the relation of Hegesippus, as preserved by Eusebius, that he was finally despatched by the blow of a fuller's club. His day, as kept by the Romans, is May 2d.

Page 92. *'An epistle of straw.'*

'*Epistola straminea,*' *a strawy epistle*, is the phrase applied by Luther to the epistle of James. The boldness, and perhaps even the rudeness of the great Reformer, qualified him to carry through his enterprise as he did, under circumstances, and in an age, which demanded not only decision, but a rough, uncompromising, unfeeling decision. Granting this to be the case, still he is not to be regarded as a pattern of christian meekness, forbearance, or charity; qualities which neither he, nor his contemporary Calvin, in any great degree possessed. Luther was more wild in his doctrine of faith than even Calvin; and he vented his spleen against good works on the excellent epistle of James, in an expression of contempt which would not be tolerated at the present day.

NOTES TO THE LIFE OF JUDE.

Page 93. *Lebbeus whose surname was Thaddeus.*

Jude is merely an English abbreviation of Judas, and Judas is only a Greek pronunciation of the old Hebrew name of Judah. It means *the praise of the Lord*. Thaddeus is derived from the same root, and has a similar signification. Lebbeus appears to mean *a man of heart, or courage*, being derived from a word signifying *the heart*.

138 NOTES.

These two last names were probably adopted to distinguish him from Judas Iscariot.

Page 94. *Other accounts of this apostle are so various and contradictory, &c.*

It is in vain to endeavour to learn anything of this apostle from the writings of the Fathers, who, as is very evident from their contradictory stories, knew nothing about him. They generally preferred, however, to record the most groundless legend, rather than to confess their ignorance. 'The men themselves,' says Dr Jortin, speaking of the Fathers, in his Remarks on Ecclesiastical History, 'usually deserve much respect, and their writings are highly useful on several accounts; but it is better to defer too little than too much to their decisions, and to the authority of *antiquity,* that *handmaid to Scripture,* as she is called. She is like *Briareus,* and has *a hundred hands,* and these hands often clash, and beat one another.'

October 28th is sacred, in the Roman Calendar, to the memory of the apostle Jude.

NOTES TO THE LIFE OF SIMON ZELOTES.

Page 96. *Canaanite is merely a Hebrew word, &c.*

'This word,' says Cave, 'has no relation to his country, or the place from whence he borrowed his original, as plainly descending from a Hebrew word which signifies *zeal,* and denotes a hot and sprightly temper. Therefore what some of the Evangelists call *Canaanite,* others, rendering the Hebrew by the Greek word, style *Simon Zelotes,* or the *Zealot.*'

Page. 97. *As far as Britain.*

'Nor could the coldness of the climate benumb his zeal,' exclaims the honest Cave, 'or hinder him from shipping himself and the christian doctrine over to the western islands, yea, even to Britain itself. Here he preached and wrought many miracles, and after infinite troubles and difficulties which he underwent, suffered martyrdom for the faith of Christ, as is not only affirmed by Nicephorus and Dorotheus, but expressly owned in the Greek Menologies, where we are told that he went at last into Britain, and having enlightened the minds of many with the doctrine of the gospel, was crucified by the infidels, and buried there.'

The two apostles Simon and Jude, are commemorated on the same day, October 28th.

NOTES TO THE LIFE OF JUDAS ISCARIOT.

Page 99. *A supper was made for him there.*

Commentators and harmonists disagree upon the question whether this supper was the same as that mentioned by Matthew as having been given in the house of Simon the leper. There are some circumstances common to both, and some peculiar to each. Macknight is confident that they were two distinct occurrences. A few of his arguments I will here repeat, which may lead the reader to further investigations.

'Although this supper (John xii. 2.) is supposed by many to have been the same with that mentioned in Matt. xxvi. 6., upon examination they will appear to have been different. This happened in the house of Lazarus; that, in the house of Simon the leper. At this, Mary, the sister of Lazarus, anointed our Lord's feet, and wiped them with her hair; at that, a woman, not named, poured the ointment on his head. Here Judas only found fault with the action; there he was seconded by some of the rest. It seems all the disciples but Judas had let this first anointing pass without censure. But when they saw so expensive a compliment repeated, and that within a few days the one of the other, they joined with him in blaming the woman, and might think themselves warranted to do so, as they knew that their Master was not delighted with luxuries of any kind.' Again he says, 'The anointing, after which Judas bargained with the priests, happened only two days before the Passover, and consequently was different from that mentioned by John, which was six days before that solemnity.'

'Thus it evidently appears,' he proceeds, 'that our Lord was anointed with spikenard three different times during the course of his ministry; once in the house of Simon the Pharisee, once in the house of Lazarus, and once in the house of Simon the leper. That this honor should have been done him so often, needs not be thought strange; for in those countries it was common at entertainments to pour fragrant oils on the heads of such guests as they designed to distinguish with marks of extraordinary respect. The custom is alluded to, Psal. xlv. 7. "God hath anointed thee with the oil of gladness above thy fellows." Where this piece of civility was showed, it was an expression of the highest complacency, and produced great gladness in the person who was the object of it.'

Page 99. *'And bare off what was put therein.'*
In our English bible it is, 'and bare what was therein;' a translation which does not seem to give the true

meaning of the passage, though the Greek verb admits of both senses.

Page 103. *A sum not more than about a third of what the ointment had cost.*

The value of the ointment was three hundred pence; the wages of treachery were thirty pieces of silver. The pence are supposed to be the Roman denarii, and a denarius is estimated at seven pence halfpenny, English money; at which rate the whole cost of the ointment would be over nine pounds sterling. The pieces of silver were probably the Jewish shekels, each of which was of a weight equivalent to about two shillings and threepence; amounting in all to between three and four pounds. A different reckoning, however, has been adopted by some, as appears from the following passage from Jeremy Taylor's Life of Christ, which I quote at length, as containing other opinions on this subject, and as being also a tolerable specimen of that writer's style. It will be perceived that the bishop takes it for granted that Mary Magdalen was the woman who anointed our Lord.

'It is not intimated,' says Taylor, 'in the history of the life of Jesus, that Judas had any malice against the person of Christ; for when afterward he saw the matter was to end in the death of his Lord, he repented; but a base and unworthy spirit of covetousness possessed him; and the relics of indignation for missing the price of the ointment which the holy Magdalen had poured upon his feet, burnt in his bowels with a secret, dark, melancholic fire, and made an eruption into an act which all the ages of the world could never parallel. They appointed him for hire thirty pieces; and some say that every piece did in value equal ten ordinary current deniers; and so Judas was satisfied by receiving the worth of the three hundred pence at which he valued the nard pistick. But hereafter let no Christian be ashamed to be despised and undervalued; for he will hardly meet so great a reproach as to have so disproportioned a price set upon his life as was upon the holy Jesus. St Mary Magdalen thought it not good enough to aneal his sacred feet; Judas thought it a sufficient price for his head; for covetousness aims at base and low purchases, whilst holy love is great and comprehensive as the bosom of Heaven, and aims at nothing that is less than infinite.'

Page 104. *The next that we hear of him is at the last supper.*

That is, the supper of the Passover. It has been disputed, whether Judas was or was not present when Jesus instituted his own supper, at the time of this feast; and it is a very difficult point to determine. 'However it was,' observes the author from whom I quoted last, 'Christ, who was Lord of the sacraments, might dispense it as he pleased.'

Page 109. *The lot fell upon Matthias.*

Nothing is particularly related of this apostle in the sacred books. The most probable account of him is, that he preached in Cappadocia, and suffered martyrdom, by the cross, in Colchis. There is another history by an author of no great credit, which relates that he preached the gospel in Macedonia; 'where the Gentiles, to make an experiment of his faith and integrity, gave him a poisonous and intoxicating potion, which he cheerfully drank off, in the name of Christ, without the least prejudice to himself; and that when the same potion had deprived above two hundred and fifty of their sight, he, laying his hands upon them, restored them to their sight;—with a great deal more of the same stamp,' says Cave, ' which I have neither faith enough to believe, nor leisure enough to relate.'

The Romans commemorate Matthias on the 24th of February.

NOTES TO THE CONCLUDING REMARKS.

Page 110. *The apostles were all Galileans.*

Seven of them, Peter and Andrew, James and John, Philip, Bartholomew, and Matthew, are expressly stated in the Gospels to have belonged to the district of Galilee. The same is in the highest degree probable of all the rest, with the exception, perhaps, of Judas Iscariot. We find that the eleven, after Jesus had ascended into heaven before their sight, were thus spoken to by the two angels; ' Ye men of Galilee, why stand ye gazing up into heaven?' And at the day of Pentecost, when they received the gift of tongues, the people who were present, exclaimed, ' Behold, are not all these who speak Galileans?' Indeed, so many of the first disciples of Christ were from Galilee, that they were all called Galileans at first, as we learn from contemporary historians.

Page 112. *One was a publican.*

It is a habit among many of the Fathers, and other writers on these subjects, to assert that Matthew was rich, in order to magnify the sacrifice which he made in leaving all to follow Jesus. But there is not the least ground in scripture for supposing that he formed an exception to the general poverty, or at any rate, very moderate circumstances of the other apostles. He was able, to be sure, to give a supper, at which some Pharisees were present, who were not likely to honor with their presence the house of a poor man; but he might have done this, and yet not have been very rich.

Page 120. *And we humbly pray to God, &c.*

As I have, in these notes, mentioned the days on which the several apostles are commemorated by the Roman or Western Church, I hope it will not be thought irrelevant to my subject, to introduce here the collects, or short petitions, which are used by the English Church on those Saints' days. Though we may not keep the days ourselves, nor attach to them any peculiar sacredness or obligation whatever, yet these prayers, still used by a great part of the christian world, and of venerable antiquity, may serve to impress on our minds the examples of holy life which have been presented in this volume, and thus form to it an appropriate and useful conclusion.

COLLECT FOR SAINT PETER'S DAY.

O Almighty God, who by thy Son Jesus Christ didst give to thy apostle Saint Peter many excellent gifts, and commandedst him earnestly to feed thy flock; make, we beseech thee, all pastors diligently to preach thy holy word, and the people obediently to follow the same, that they may receive the crown of everlasting glory, through Jesus Christ our Lord.

COLLECT FOR SAINT ANDREW'S DAY.

ALMIGHTY God, who didst give such grace unto thy holy apostle Saint Andrew, that he readily obeyed the calling of thy Son Jesus Christ, and followed him without delay; grant unto us all, that we, being called by thy holy word, may forthwith give up ourselves obediently to fulfil thy holy commandments, through the same Jesus Christ our Lord.

COLLECT FOR SAINT JAMES'* DAY.

Grant, O merciful God, that as thine holy apostle Saint James, leaving his father and all that he had, without delay was obedient unto the calling of thy Son Jesus Christ, and followed him; so we, forsaking all worldly and carnal affections, may be evermore ready to follow thy holy commandments, through Jesus Christ our Lord.

COLLECT FOR SAINT JOHN THE EVANGELIST'S DAY.

Merciful Lord, we beseech thee to cast thy bright beams of light upon thy church, that it, being enlightened by the doctrine of thy blessed apostle and evangelist Saint John, may so walk in the light of thy truth, that it may at length attain to the light of everlasting life, through Jesus Christ our Lord.

COLLECT FOR SAINT PHILIP AND SAINT JAMES'† DAY.

O Almighty God, whom truly to know is everlasting life; grant us perfectly to know thy Son Jesus Christ to be the way, the truth, and the life, that following the steps of thy holy apostles Saint Philip and Saint James, we may steadfastly walk in the way that leadeth to eternal life, through the same thy Son Jesus Christ our Lord.

COLLECT FOR SAINT BARTHOLOMEW'S DAY.

O Almighty and everlasting God, who didst give to thine apostle Bartholomew grace truly to believe and preach thy word; grant, we beseech thee, unto thy church, to love that word which he believed, and both to preach and receive the same, through Jesus Christ our Lord.

* The Greater.   † The Less.

COLLECT FOR SAINT THOMAS' DAY.

Almighty and everlasting God, who, for the more confirmation of the faith didst suffer thy holy apostle Thomas to be doubtful in thy Son's resurrection; grant us so perfectly, and without all doubt to believe in thy Son Jesus Christ, that our faith in thy sight may never be reproved. Hear us, O Lord, in the name of Jesus Christ, through whom to thee be all honor and glory, now and for evermore.

COLLECT FOR SAINT MATTHEW'S DAY.

O Almighty God, who by thy blessed Son didst call Matthew from the receipt of custom, to be an apostle and evangelist; grant us grace to forsake all covetous desires and inordinate love of riches, and to follow the same thy Son Jesus Christ our Lord, who liveth and reigneth with thee, world without end.

COLLECT FOR SAINT SIMON AND SAINT JUDE'S DAY.

O Almighty God, who hast built thy church upon the foundation of the apostles and prophets, Jesus Christ himself being the head corner stone; grant us so to be joined together in unity of spirit by their doctrine, that we may be made an holy temple acceptable unto thee, through Jesus Christ our Lord.

COLLECT FOR SAINT MATTHIAS' DAY.

O Almighty God, who into the place of the traitor Judas didst choose thy faithful servant Matthias to be of the number of the twelve apostles; grant that thy church, being alway preserved from false apostles, may be ordered and guided by faithful and true pastors, through Jesus Christ our Lord.

A

HYMN

FOR SAINT STEPHEN'S AND OTHER SAINTS' DAYS;

BY BISHOP HEBER.

The Son of God goes forth to war,
   A kingly crown to gain;
His blood-red banner streams afar!
   Who follows in his train?

Who best can drink his cup of woe,
   Triumphant over pain,
Who patient bears his cross below,
   He follows in his train!

The martyr first, whose eagle eye
   Could pierce beyond the grave;
Who saw his Master in the sky,
   And called on him to save.

Like him, with pardon on his tongue
   In midst of mortal pain,
He prayed for them that did the wrong!
   Who follows in his train?

A glorious band, the chosen few,
   On whom the spirit came;
Twelve valiant saints, their hope they knew,
   And mocked the cross and flame.

They met the tyrant's brandished steel,
  The lion's gory mane;
They bowed their necks the death to feel!
  Who follows in their train?

A noble army—men and boys,
  The matron and the maid,
Around the Saviour's throne rejoice,
  In robes of light arrayed.

They climbed the steep ascent of Heaven,
  Through peril, toil, and pain!
O God! to us may grace be given
  To follow in their train!

THE END.